W9-BAY-301

FLORET FARM'S

A Year in Flowers

Designing

Gorgeous

Arrangements

for Every Season

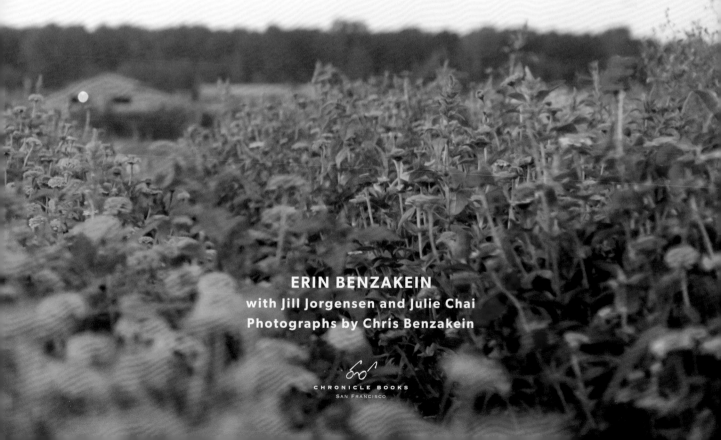

ERIN BENZAKEIN
with Jill Jorgensen and Julie Chai
Photographs by Chris Benzakein

CHRONICLE BOOKS
SAN FRANCISCO

Library of Congress Cataloging-in-Publication Data:

Names: Benzakein, Erin, author. | Jorgensen, Jill,
author. | Chai, Julie, author.
Title: Floret Farm's a year in flowers / Erin Benzakein
with Jill Jorgensen and Julie Chai.
Other titles: Year in flowers
Description: San Francisco : Chronicle Books, [2020]
Identifiers: LCCN 2019015714 | ISBN 9781452172897
(hardcover : alk. paper)
Subjects: LCSH: Flower arrangement. |
Cut flowers. | Bouquets.
Classification: LCC SB449 .B423 2020 | DDC 745.92—
dc23 LC record available at
https://lccn.loc.gov/2019015714

Manufactured in China.
Design by Vanessa Dina.

10 9 8 7 6 5 4 3 2

Chronicle books and gifts are available at special
quantity discounts to corporations, professional
associations, literacy programs, and other organiza-
tions. For details and discount information, please
contact our premiums department at corporatesales@
chroniclebooks.com or at 1-800-759-0190.

Chronicle Books LLC
680 Second Street
San Francisco, CA 94107
www.chroniclebooks.com

A Year in Flowers

To all of the magical souls who so patiently
shared their time and wisdom with me.
Your overwhelming generosity has altered the course of my life.
I will try my best to pay it forward, always.

My Journey with Flowers

Much of my childhood was spent at my great-grandparents' country home, and at an early age I inherited from them a deep love of nature. From then on I dreamed of living in the country, where I'd grow my own vegetables, raise chickens, and plant a small orchard. So in 2001, my husband, Chris, and I left the hustle of city life in Seattle and moved to a small farm in Washington's Skagit Valley to pursue a slower, simpler, more intentional lifestyle where we could raise our children surrounded by nature. Shortly after we arrived, a generous neighbor brought over his tractor to till a plot of ground so I could finally have the garden of my dreams.

Chris kept his job in the city and continued to commute back and forth for the first few years. I was home with two small children, feeling incredibly lonely and restless. I filled my days taking care of Elora and Jasper while simultaneously trying to figure out what I wanted to be when I grew up. To keep my mind occupied, I tried out numerous business ideas to see what would stick, including planting an heirloom cider orchard (I didn't take into account that it would be at least five years before my first viable harvest). I raised more than a hundred chickens in our backyard for a rainbow egg business, but the birds kept escaping from their coop, and I would get angry calls from our neighbors daily. I even tried my hand at growing miniature vegetables for local customers, but quickly realized that it takes a lot of baby zucchini to make $5. I tried just about everything in my quest to find something I could do while raising young kids that related to nature and allowed me to work from home.

Along the way, I added flowers to my garden and started selling the extra blooms. Unlike all of the other things that I made or grew, flowers had the power to stir such deep emotion. Every time I delivered my homegrown blooms, complete strangers would open up and share the most beautiful stories with me. Almost every recipient had a flower memory that they could recall as if it were yesterday. It wasn't until I started sharing flowers, which I'd grown myself and made into bouquets, that I felt like I had finally found my calling.

From that season forward, every waking minute was devoted to the garden. I was obsessed. But I knew very little about flower

farming. I spent nearly every evening and weekend camped out in online chat rooms, having long question-and-answer sessions with flower growers across the country. We were all so determined to help put locally grown flowers on the map that any sense of competition was thrown out the window, and farmers freely shared trade secrets. It was because of this supportive community that I learned so much about growing, so quickly.

Learning about floral design, however, proved to be much more difficult. Every book I could get my hands on featured tightly packed, contrived arrangements filled with imported blooms that were completely out of season. The ingredients in those displays looked nothing like the ones growing in my garden—their uniform color and stick-straight stems were devoid of any personality or magic.

Around this time, a handful of innovative designers began approaching flowers in a completely new and unexpected way, using ingredients common in home gardens but not typically thought of as bouquet material. This approach, which has come to be known as natural floral design, focuses on what's in season and embraces a plant's natural habit and subtle coloring. Designers intentionally stagger bloom height for a looser look, so the finished arrangement appears to be growing out of the vase. Because natural floral design celebrates the best of what's in season, these arrangements capture a fleeting moment in time. I tore out magazine pictures of their work, pinned them to the wall in my garage, and began trying to mimic their style. I just couldn't figure out how they achieved such stunning results.

Learning this style was incredibly frustrating because I didn't understand how the bouquets could simultaneously look so loose and lush and still stay intact in the vase. Every time I tried to recreate something I'd seen, my arrangements would end up either looking way too full and messy or completely falling apart. For every beautiful arrangement I made, there were half a dozen discards that ended up in the compost pile. I spent more tearful evenings in the garage trying to master natural floral design than I'd like to remember.

Back then, I didn't understand that in order to create natural-looking bouquets, I needed to master several key components: using the right supplies, having the right mix of ingredients, and following a process when arranging. Unfortunately, this information was not widely known or accessible—if you didn't know someone who could teach you, the only way to figure it out was through frustrating trial and error.

But over time and after tons of practice, I slowly started to find my way. I reached out to people whose work I admired, cultivated relationships, and had the great fortune of studying with many of my floral heroes. I'd fallen in love with both floral design and flower farming and wanted to combine them, but all the experts told me it couldn't be done: growers had no business arranging flowers, and florists couldn't rely completely on seasonal material. Most florists were unaware of the huge range of ingredients available locally, so they continued buying what they were familiar with—like standard hothouse roses, calla lilies, and hydrangeas—most of which came from outside the country. Local farmers played it safe by cultivating well-known varieties, not realizing there was a huge market for their farm-fresh bouquets and hard-to-ship blooms like sweet peas and dahlias.

I was determined to bridge the two worlds, and I found the most effective way to do this was by showing people what was possible using local flowers. I experimented year after year, perfecting

my growing techniques, always sharing what I learned along the way. I designed with herbs, vegetables, fruit on the branch, and seedpods to see how they performed as cut material. I relentlessly practiced making arrangements, and for nine months—an entire spring through autumn—each week I met my goal of making one glorious bouquet using only seasonal material that I had grown or gathered, and I shared it on my blog. This exercise served two purposes: first, to continue honing my design skills, and second, to challenge the notion that you can't make stunning arrangements using only locally sourced foliage and blooms.

I was absolutely blown away by the outpouring of positive feedback, and after many requests I eventually opened up our farm to host workshops and teach others what I had learned. As a farmer-florist—a term that describes people like me who specialize in both growing and arranging with seasonal flowers—I taught about both small-scale organic flower farming and seasonally based floral design. Budding and established growers, as well as designers from all over the world, made the pilgrimage to our tiny two-acre farm. Over the course of several years, we welcomed more than five hundred flower lovers to learn with us. We turned attendees loose in our fields to cut to their heart's content. Many of them were moved to tears because even though some were floral designers who worked with flowers every day, they had never seen a real working farm or had the opportunity to harvest from the field. It was the first time I had seen our flowers so deeply appreciated and elevated in such a reverent and refined way. It was life altering for all of us involved, and I realized that we had something really special to share with a wider audience.

Through teaching these workshops, I discovered that nearly everyone struggled with the same things I once did when it came to making bouquets: how to approach color, basic mechanics, proper ingredient selection, and most importantly, how to build confidence. From watching hundreds of students learn how to create floral arrangements, we developed a tried-and-true, straightforward process that took away the guesswork and resulted in beautiful bouquets every time. With a basic recipe to follow, students were finally able to relax and focus on cultivating their own personal style, and to enjoy the seasonal ingredients they were working with.

Along this journey I have had the honor of connecting with thousands of people, and nearly every one of them has had a flower story to share. Whether we realize it or not, flowers have touched all of our lives in deep and personal way. They mark life's important milestones, including birth, marriage, motherhood, anniversaries, holidays, and even our final days. Witnessing the transformative magic of flowers has been one of my greatest joys—and that's what I want to share with you. In this book, I detail the basics of getting started with floral design, key ingredients, essential techniques, and ideas for every season.

I learned much of what I know because so many generous souls were willing to pass along their knowledge to me, and in the same spirit of sharing, I offer what I've learned to you. My hope is that this book will inspire you to make your own flower memories and cultivate more beauty in your life.

Getting Started

Before you dive into flower arranging, it's important to set yourself up for success by designating a workspace and gathering all the supplies and vessels you'll need. With that taken care of, when it comes time to choose your flowers and prep them for arranging, knowing what to look for in your ingredients and how to treat them will ensure that your bouquets last as long as possible.

Setting Up Your Space

Whether you're making a casual posy for your kitchen table or a series of centerpieces for an event or a holiday, it's important to have a dedicated workspace, even if it's temporary, where you can create freely. You don't need a ton of room, but you do want a place that's stocked with all your tools and supplies, with enough space to accommodate your spreading out, spilling water, and dropping leaves and stems on the floor.

In the early years, I had a little table in the corner of our covered back porch where I made bouquets. On cold blustery days, it wasn't the coziest place to work, but I could leave all my tools and materials out and make a big, beautiful mess whenever I wanted. As my hobby grew, I eventually claimed the back half of our garage for flower arranging. Then, when my bouquet making turned into a business, I gradually relocated all of my husband's tools into the shed and made the garage my own, added standing-height countertops, a stainless steel sink with hot running water, plenty of shelves for all of my vases, and a walk-in cooler. I whitewashed the walls, and my mom sewed me cute bunting that we hung from the rafters. Now it's one of my favorite places to work.

Your setup can be quite simple. My mom, for example, uses a kitchen cupboard to store her collection of vases and keeps her snips, buckets, and flower food under the sink. She can be set up in just a few minutes and make an easy-to-clean mess on the kitchen floor. When you're working inside the house, you can simplify cleanup by laying a shower curtain or tarp on the floor before you start; this will contain anything that falls, and it makes cleanup easy.

When setting up your workspace, you'll want all your tools, supplies, buckets, and vases within easy reach, with ready access to running water. You'll also want a standing-height table or counter to prevent back and neck pain. If you don't already have a surface that tall, you can raise a folding banquet table using pieces of PVC 12 to 18 in (30 to 45 cm) long slipped under the feet. And if your flower-arranging area is tucked into a dark corner or basement, make sure that you have adequate lighting—it's essential that you be able to see what you're making. You can pick up inexpensive LED shop lights at most hardware stores that will sufficiently brighten dim spaces.

If you don't have room to carve out a permanent work area, a folding table—set up in a shady spot if outside—will do the trick. You can elevate your arrangements on upside-down buckets so you don't have to hunch over while you work.

It can feel indulgent to carve out a spot for yourself, but it's essential to the creative process to have a dedicated space where you can design whenever inspiration strikes.

Floral Toolbox

I always keep the following tools and supplies within easy reach in my studio.

RIBBON I have a large collection of varying widths and colors of both silk and double-faced satin ribbon. This is a must for wedding work.

PEARL-HEADED STICK PINS/STRAIGHT PINS These are essential for securing ribbon to bouquets and for pinning on boutonnieres.

PADDLE WIRE Available on a continuous spool, this wire is ideal for making wreaths and garlands.

OASIS FLORAL ADHESIVE This versatile waterproof adhesive, commonly referred to as cold glue, bonds quickly to all surfaces. It's perfect for adhering fresh or dried flowers and ribbon to any surface without the use of tape or wire.

RUBBER BANDS Number 19 is the perfect size for bunching flowers and securing bouquets.

WATERPROOF FLORAL TAPE This sturdy tape is perfect for securing chicken wire and floral pillows in a vase and wrapping bouquets for extra support. The ¼ in (6 mm) size is my favorite.

FLORAL STEM WRAP This tape, which adheres to itself when gently stretched, is ideal for boutonnieres, corsages, and flower crowns. I find the light green to be the most versatile.

PAPER-COVERED WIRE Available in green, brown, and tan, this handy wire makes the perfect base for a flower crown and is what I use to attach garlands to banisters and doorways.

COTTON TWINE This adds a natural look when wrapping boutonnieres and tying bouquets.

JUTE TWINE Use it to tie bouquets and make garlands.

GLOVES Lightweight nitrile gloves are my daily go-to because they are durable, breathable, and can be tossed in the washing machine. They are great to have on hand when working with thorny materials like bells of Ireland and roses, and they protect hands from the irritating sap of euphorbia.

BRASS CUFF Also known as a jewelry blank, this simple cuff base has revolutionized the way I make corsages. Flowers and textural ingredients can be glued to these stylish bracelets with Oasis floral adhesive.

ROSE STRIPPER This handy tool makes removing thorns from roses and other prickly stems fast and easy.

FLOWER SNIPS Lightweight needle-nose flower snips are my go-to for everyday harvesting and flower arranging. They work well for both delicate blooms like sweet peas and thicker stems like dahlias and zinnias. They are perfectly shaped to rest in the palm of your hand, so you can harvest for hours without getting a sore wrist.

PRUNERS A pair of heavy-duty pruners is a must-have when working with woody-stemmed plants. My favorite brand is ARS, because their blades are chrome plated to resist rust and their handles are ergonomically designed especially for smaller hands.

SCISSORS It's essential to designate a pair of fabric scissors for ribbon only to preserve the blade's sharp edge. I tie a piece of ribbon to the handle of mine as a reminder to not use them for paper or wire, which can dull the blade.

STRAIGHT FLORAL WIRE These precut pieces of wire are perfect for wiring individual ingredients for wearable flowers and attaching bundles of interesting ingredients to wreaths and garlands. It comes in many sizes; my favorite is 22-gauge. The most common length is 18 in (45 cm).

APRON Working with flowers is messy. When arranging, I wear a half apron with pockets to protect my clothes and keep supplies handy.

19

Floral Mechanics Supplies

Nontoxic mechanics, most of which are reusable, are essential for natural floral design. A collection of different options will help you lay the foundation for beautiful arrangements that stay in place.

PIN FROGS One of the best tools in the flower-arranging arsenal, this allows you to securely arrange heavy, woody branches even in shallow vessels.

KRAFT PAPER Having a roll of this versatile paper on hand allows you to quickly and easily wrap gift bouquets and pad arrangements for delivery.

CHICKEN WIRE An eco-friendly alternative to toxic flower foam, a ball of chicken wire inserted into a vase provides a sturdy framework to keep heavier stems upright. I like to use the green coated wire whenever possible because it is less prone to rusting.

FLORAL ADHESIVE CLAY This waterproof adhesive secures flower frogs to the bottom of vases. It's available in green or white; I prefer Floralife Sure-Stick in green because it is the most durable and long lasting.

CAGE FROGS This style of frog is ideal for larger arrangements with thick heavy stems. I love to use them when working with lilies and peonies because the stems stay where I want them and they are easy to slip in and out.

FLORAL HYDRATION STEM WRAP I lovingly refer to this awesome invention by Eco Fresh Bouquet as the "flower diaper." These handy hydrating wraps are perfect for wrapping stem ends to keep gift bouquets fresh out of water for many hours.

WATERPROOF FLORAL TAPE This sturdy tape is perfect for securing chicken wire in a vase and wrapping bouquets for extra support. The ¼ in (6 mm) size by Oasis is my favorite. It is also available in a ½ in (12 mm) width.

HOLLY HEIDER CHAPPLE PILLOW An eco-friendly and more effective alternative to floral foam, these reusable plastic grids mimic the grid created by chicken wire, but without the hassle. They come in four different sizes that can be nestled or taped into any vase of your choice, allowing you to place stems at an angle and create loose, lush arrangements. They're a great alternative to chicken wire pillows, especially if you're making a lot of arrangements.

WIRE WREATH FRAME Available in multiple sizes from most craft stores, these provide a sturdy base for wreath making.

HAIRPIN FROGS This style of floral frog is my very favorite because it allows you to insert stems at any angle and create lush, trailing bouquets.

23

Using Flower Frogs

I have three favorite styles that I use most often, each of which holds stems a bit differently. The pin frog, a flat, heavy metal base covered in pin-like spikes, holds larger stems and heavy, fruit-laden branches in place with ease. The hairpin frog is covered in metal hooks into which you can slip stems at any angle, including the sides, holding them perfectly in place. The cage frog has a wire grid that accommodates thicker stems or bunches of slender stems inserted in the grid openings.

Securing a Flower Frog

1 Tear off a generous length of floral adhesive clay, enough to cover the perimeter of the flower frog base. Twist and press until the entire outer edge is covered, essentially making a waterproof seal.

2 Set the flower frog, adhesive side down, in the center of the vessel. Press to adhere.

3 Once the frog is in place, use a folded dish towel to protect your hand while you apply pressure to the frog for 10 to 20 seconds. This ensures that a good seal is formed. Let the adhesive clay cure for 20 to 30 minutes before adding water.

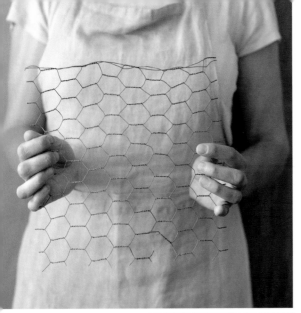

Making a Chicken Wire Pillow

1 Using wire cutters or a designated pair of pruners, cut a square of chicken wire that's roughly twice as big as the space you intend to fill.

2 Being careful not to poke yourself, fold the corners of the wire under, wadding as you go to create a pillow-like shape.

3 Nestle the pillow into your vessel and secure in place by making an *X* with waterproof floral tape across the top.

Vessels

When it comes to choosing a vessel, it's important to understand that each vase lends itself to certain types of arrangements. For example, low, wide bowls are ideal for centerpieces, whereas taller, footed urns are well suited for dramatic, grand statement pieces. So your container choice is as important to the overall look as the ingredients themselves.

Rather than amassing a huge collection of vases in all shapes and sizes, I recommend building a collection of favorites that support your style of arranging. Over the years, I've picked up most of my vases at thrift shops and antique stores and from artisan potters. I periodically go through what I have and get rid of anything that

SMALL BOTTLES AND JARS These are ideal for displaying individual stems or a collection of small bundles of flowers. They look right at home on a windowsill, arrayed down a long table, or displaying a vignette (an arrangement that makes the most of a small quantity of flowers).

CONFIT JAR This shape lends itself to a full arrangement because the neck of the vase holds the stems upright. The larger size is perfect for displaying flowers en masse (in a big, showy display highlighting a single flower type); the smaller version makes a more traditional, rounded bouquet. With this shape of vessel, you can get away without using a flower frog or chicken wire.

COMPOTE BOWL To create a low centerpiece, it's important to choose a shallow bowl (with or without a foot) that has a wide flared top and is at least 4 in (10 cm) deep so that the stems are submerged in adequate water. This shape allows you to create an arrangement with stems placed horizontally for a lush look that doesn't obstruct views.

I haven't used in a while. I definitely subscribe to quality over quantity when it comes to vessels.

In most cases, I recommend you choose a vase that's flared, with an opening wider than the base, to allow flowers to spill out over the top. Stay away from glass cubes, cheap glass vases with pinched centers, and anything resembling a fishbowl. These styles are nearly impossible to arrange in because they work against the natural, loose style that I teach about in this book.

It's also nice to keep a supply of inexpensive glass vessels, such as mason jars, on hand for flowers that you're giving away. That way you don't have to lend your favorite vases and then track them down later. Here are the shapes that I use most often.

TAPER This form is extremely easy to arrange into. Larger taper-style vessels can be used for large-scale arranging, similar to an urn, but the result will be less formal. Smaller taper-style arrangements have a casual, carefree feel.

URN Its heft makes an urn perfect for large, dramatic arrangements. As much as possible, choose one that has a foot with a diameter wider than the top so it can support the weight of a finished arrangement.

CROCK This type of vessel is ideal for displaying tall blooms and large branches, since its heavy bottom ensures that the arrangement won't tip over.

Sourcing

For loose, garden-style arrangements, the quality of the material matters, so I strongly urge you to source your ingredients from as nearby as possible. Flowers are just like food: the best results always come from using local, seasonal ingredients picked at their prime. When you're sourcing materials locally, not only are they fresher and more vibrant, but they're also more likely to have appealing natural characteristics like arching stems, a graceful, scrambling habit, and unique coloring. Most of the flowers that you find at the wholesaler, grocery store, or corner market—bred to travel halfway around the world out of water—are devoid of personality, with stick-straight stems and little fragrance. They don't lend themselves to the bouquet styles you'll see in this book.

As you look at fresh local plants more closely, you'll start noticing their subtle details. You'll learn to celebrate, and seek out, what you may have previously thought of as imperfections, like curved branching stems, mottled foliage, and uneven bloom coloring. The level of variation in the natural world is far more beautiful than anything that you're going to find in the store. So, when sourcing flowers and foliage for your arrangements, try to stay as close to home as possible.

In my experience, you can find lovely local ingredients in spring, summer, and autumn (and even winter may surprise you). So pay attention to what's growing around you. If you have a yard, there may be a bounty of things you could be picking that you simply haven't discovered yet. Look to the wild spaces and hedgerows where many treasures can be foraged responsibly and yield far more beautiful and interesting results than you'll get with conventional imported blooms.

Floral Wholesaler

One of the most common ways to buy flowers is from a wholesaler. Floral wholesale houses are typically located in large cities, in grittier, industrial parts of town. The first time I visited a wholesaler, I had a mental vision of an indoor farmers market, each display brimming with the most beautiful fresh flowers imaginable. When I arrived, it was exactly the opposite of my fantasy: a massive, dimly lit warehouse with row after row of floral supplies—including glittered branches, silk flowers, potted plants, and scented pinecones—with a very small fresh flower area. I got there a few hours before closing, and anything worth choosing had been picked over. All that was left were imported, cardboard-wrapped roses, gerbera daisies, cruddy old eucalyptus, and plumosa fern. I quickly realized that, to successfully shop there, I'd have to learn the rules.

To shop at the wholesale house, you'll need a business license. Set up an account before you go, and sign up for their weekly availability email list so that you can start learning about what's happening at the market and get a sense of pricing. Before buying anything, I'd also suggest visiting during one of the slower times, often later in the day, to get your bearings and the lay of the land. Find the friendliest face, introduce yourself, and ask them to walk you through the process of doing business with them.

For the best selection, you need to arrive very early, typically around 4 a.m. Bring a list of what you're looking for, because it's easy to get overwhelmed by the commotion and choices, and you may forget what you came for or buy too much. It's kind of like the advice to not go grocery shopping when you're hungry. Take your time and examine each bunch closely. Many of the blooms at the wholesale house are at least two weeks old by the time they arrive, so you need to inspect for signs of mold and rot. Fresh flowers have plump, vibrant buds, and the foliage on the lower part of the stem is still green. If the lower leaves are turning yellow or brown, the flower heads are wilted and droopy, or the water smells, don't buy them.

Most wholesalers have a decent selection of local product, so be sure to ask your salesperson which varieties are coming from nearby farms.

The local product tends to fly out the door, so be sure to snag it early.

The wholesale house generally has a very good selection of professional-grade products that cost half to a third of what you would pay at your local craft store, so it's a great place to buy supplies including floral preservative, wire, ribbon, waterproof tape, and vases. For the best pricing, purchase supplies in bulk and containers by the case. I often go in with some friends and share bulk quantities of frequently used items.

A few things to note: Treat sellers' flowers with great care. When lifting out bunches to inspect, make sure that the water is not dripping all over the other bunches. When replacing an inspected bunch in the bucket, make sure you submerge the stem ends in the water and you don't damage the other bunches. Be courteous and aware of your surroundings. In short, be a good customer. The people shopping the market are busy professional florists with their own deadlines. Don't block the aisle or monopolize the salespeople's time with a lot of questions; they'll have more time during nonpeak hours. The folks working the floor have to put up with a lot of drama every day, because they are dealing with high-maintenance customers. Go the extra mile to be friendly, flexible, and polite. Establishing good relationships with vendors early on will give you access to the very best of what the market has to offer in the long run.

29

Local Farms

There are few things I love more than buying flowers and foliage from local growers. Even when our fields are overflowing with blooms, I never pass up an opportunity to source from other farmers. Although we all grow flowers professionally, I find that each farmer has their own niche and focus. Learn what flowers each farmer specializes in, and you'll be able to access an amazing variety of plant material all year round.

For many years we sold fresh flowers to floral designers, event planners, and brides doing their own wedding arrangements, and each week I received dozens of email inquiries asking to tour the farm, pick my brain, and shadow me for the day. They would attach a very specific wish list of flowers and foliage they wanted on a certain date, not understanding that their preferences didn't align with what would be in season at that time. At first, I was very discouraged and frustrated because the requests were impossible to meet.

But as time went on, I realized that these well-intentioned flower lovers simply needed to learn about seasonality.

Before you approach a local grower, take time to gain a basic understanding of what types of blooms can be sourced locally. For example, you're unlikely to find long-stemmed roses, tropicals, carnations, or baby's breath at most local farms. Unlike the wholesale house, where many varieties are available all year because they're shipped in from faraway places, local growers have a finite window—anywhere from two to five weeks—in which each variety is available. For example, field tulips are available only in early spring, and flowering branches bloom and fade long before summer. If your local growers send out a weekly availability list, be sure to sign up for it so that you can start learning about the bloom times for flowers in your region.

Also, farmers can't predict exactly what's going to be blooming at a specific time because the weather varies. For instance, a heat wave could run a sweet pea crop to completion in a few short weeks. In a more temperate year, that same crop could stretch over three long months. Farmers have no control over the weather, and it's nearly impossible for them to project exactly what will be available when, even two weeks into the future.

Ordering a specific list of flowers from the wholesale house is standard procedure, but when working with a local grower, you will have much more success if you're flexible and open to what they offer. You may not recognize some of these ingredients at first, but trust me, what they grow will far surpass your wildest expectations. When working with flower farmers, the most useful information you can give them is your pick-up date, the number of bunches you need, and a loose color palette. With those details, they can select a beautiful array of blooms and foliage that will take your work to the next level and set it apart from standard floral fare.

If you're a floral designer and know what events you have on the books for the coming year, you'll find that many flower farmers are more than willing to custom grow many of the staple ingredients used in your weekly arrangements. For example, a local designer and I got together one winter and looked at all of his upcoming weddings, including the number of arrangements and color palettes. I planted a section of our field in foliage and fillers that he loved and were versatile enough to work for all of his events. This gave him access to the freshest, most unusual product, and I was guaranteed a standing order each week. It was a win for both of us. This type of collaboration is successful only when designers are open minded and flexible, while committing to purchasing what the farmer planted for them. Cutting back orders at the last minute is a quick way to jeopardize the relationship.

Late spring through early autumn is the busiest time on a farm, so if you want to connect with local growers for more than ordering fresh flowers at that time of year, I recommend contacting them in the off season; winter is the perfect time to get together for coffee or chat on the phone.

It's important to note that farmers are among the hardest working and busiest people on the planet, and during peak season it's just not possible for them to give tours. If you visit then, plan on supporting their work with an order so they can continue growing the gorgeous flowers you seek. Be mindful of the time it takes to work out a custom order by phone or email, and do so only if you're planning on making a substantial purchase. Speaking from my own experience serving designers, your local flower farm will appreciate your spending at least $250 on any special order.

If your budget is smaller, or you're simply looking for everyday quantities of beautiful locally grown blooms, check out the farmers markets in your area. These are wonderful places to discover and connect with regional growers. Once you've experienced the local difference, you'll never go back.

You won't find a better product or kinder people to spend your budget on than local flower farmers. Once you establish a good relationship, they will be your very best allies and the ones harvesting dahlias after dark with headlamps to make sure you can delight your bride on her wedding day.

To find flower farms in your area, see "Resources" on page 302 for a list of directories.

31

Grow Your Own

One of the most delightful and rewarding things you can do is grow your own cut flowers. Few pursuits are more satisfying than going to your garden and harvesting armloads of fresh blooms that you have nurtured. But many gardeners have been conditioned to resist the desire to pick from their blooming plants and instead leave them to put on a flowery display. I had been gardening for years before I was bitten by the floral design bug, and I had to unlearn much of what I'd been taught about how to interact with plants in the garden. As a child I was allowed to pick weeds in the alley or blooms from the wildflower patch along the side of the house. But I was never allowed to clip from the manicured beds that surrounded our house. When I finally had a plot of my own and started making flower arrangements, I really had to overcome my learned hesitation to cut from the garden.

One way I did this was by planting a cutting garden in a section of our backyard devoted solely to plants grown to be harvested. Having the freedom to pick to my heart's content without diminishing the display was life changing. I could go out and pick whatever I wanted and bring it into the house to enjoy up close, watching a flower's full life cycle right before my eyes, from bud to bloom to slow decay. It was eye opening, and it stirred an awakening to the natural world and my place in it.

In my previous book, *Floret Farm's Cut Flower Garden*, I detail how you can successfully grow your own bouquet materials. Even if you have only a raised bed on the side of your house or a patio garden, you can successfully grow a cutting garden. And when it comes to homegrown ingredients, think outside the box. Don't limit yourself to just flowers—fruit, vegetables, and herbs are great candidates for arrangements as well. I love the airy white flowers of bolted cilantro, stems of raspberries, and clusters of tomatoes for tucking into centerpieces.

Forage

Foraging is a great way to get your hands on an abundance of interesting free material to round out your arrangements, but this can be a sensitive topic. By no means am I encouraging stealing or trespassing. I actively forage for a lot of material throughout the year, especially when it comes to wreath making or for large events, and I'm always conscious of being respectful and responsible to people, properties, and the plants.

There are so many overgrown and abandoned properties that offer a treasure trove of foliage and flowers to harvest from, and it's a shame to see all of this great material go to waste. Once you start looking, you'll notice just how many deserted areas have foraging potential. Some of my favorite places to frequent are derelict buildings, the ditches along back roads, and friends' rural properties.

Of course, you should never pick from private properties without permission. If someone were to come on your land and harvest without your consent, you would be rightfully upset. Always ask first. I've knocked on a lot of doors asking the owners for permission to pick a handful or two of a coveted ingredient, and I've never been turned down. I always offer to pay them or trade them something in return. Know that it's illegal to harvest on state lands, in parks, and in protected areas. These spaces are off-limits for a reason.

In all cases, respect the plant you're harvesting from. Never remove more than one-third of it, and be sure to cut above a leaf node or joint so that the plant can heal quickly and generate new growth. Always use pruners; never rip or tear, as that will hinder the plant's ability to heal. Finally, leave no trace. Be mindful of your impact, both in the amount of material you're harvesting and in how you got there, whether by foot or vehicle. If done right, it should look as if you were never there.

Caring for Cut Flowers

The summer I grew my first cutting garden, I was eager to share the bounty with family and friends. I harvested the biggest, prettiest blooms I could find, and as I arranged them, I noticed some fared better than others. While many lasted for a week or more, others wilted quickly, and some never even opened fully in the vase.

Over the years I've learned, sometimes the hard way, what it takes to keep each type of flower fresh for as long as possible. I still remember my heart sinking when I discovered the lilacs I had painstakingly harvested one evening for an important event the next day had wilted in their buckets by morning. Or the time a florist called in a panic because the poppies I had just delivered for her biggest wedding of the year were dropping petals all over the counter. Had I better understood post-harvest care techniques, I could have avoided these failures and many more.

Knowing the proper time to cut flowers and understanding what to do with them after you've harvested them or brought them home from the market so that they last as long as possible can seem pretty complicated at first. It really is a science unto itself. If you cut too soon, some blooms will wilt or never open; cut others too late, and they will fall apart within a matter of hours. Over the last decade, I've tried every trick in the book, and even made up a few of my own, to get the maximum vase life out of each and every flower we grow. I'm thrilled to share my time-tested tips here.

HOW TO HARVEST

USE CLEAN, SHARP CLIPPERS Rusty, dull flower snips are not just frustrating to use; they can also damage stems and reduce the vase life of your blooms. Invest in a pair of high-quality clippers, clean them after each use, and sharpen them regularly.

HARVEST DURING THE COOLEST PARTS OF THE DAY Early morning or evening are the best times to cut flowers and foliage because this is when they are the most hydrated. Blooms harvested in midday heat will wilt faster and have a harder time bouncing back than those cut when it's cooler.

TAKE A BUCKET OF WATER WITH YOU INTO THE GARDEN This allows you to place cut stems in water right away. Make sure all your stem ends are well below the water line, as fresh flowers drink a lot, especially in the first few days.

CUT AT THE PROPER STAGE Each variety has its own special tricks (see the "A–Z Ingredient Guide" on page 282), but a general rule of thumb is to cut flowers when they are between one-third and halfway open. Once the bees get to your blooms, the flowers will fade much faster. For foliage, it's important to wait until the stems are mature and firm. If picked too young, they won't last long in the vase and often wilt immediately.

MAXIMIZE STEM LENGTH When harvesting, cut as long a stem as possible without disfiguring the plant. By doing so, you encourage the plant to send out more branches at the base, resulting in longer stems and more of them. Longer stems are better for arranging and command a higher price if you plan on selling them.

HOW TO CARE FOR FLOWERS AFTER HARVEST OR FROM THE MARKET

REMOVE LOWER LEAVES FROM STEMS Foliage remaining on the stem will quickly decay once it's submerged in water. The bacteria created during the decaying process can build up and prevent the stem ends from taking up water.

ALWAYS USE CLEAN BUCKETS AND VASES Thoroughly clean your vessels with hot soapy water prior to putting flowers into them. My general rule of thumb is to make sure they're clean enough to drink from. Dirt and bacteria can quickly clog flower stems, preventing them from taking up water, and will significantly shorten their vase life.

ALLOW FLOWERS TIME TO REST PRIOR TO ARRANGING THEM This process is called conditioning, and though often overlooked, it is a critical step. After cutting your flowers and foliage, place them in deep, cool water overnight (or for at least 3 to 4 hours). You'll be amazed at how some of the more wilt-prone blooms will remain perky after being conditioned.

RECUT THE STEMS Prior to arranging your flowers in a vase, cut the stem ends once more to encourage them to take up water.

KEEP YOUR FLOWERS IN A COOL SPOT, AWAY FROM FRUIT Flowers last longer when kept away from heat, bright light, and ripening fruit and vegetables, which may emit ethylene gas that can shorten vase life.

35

Hydration Categories

Many of the varieties listed in this book fall into one of the following hydration categories, which are indicated in the "A–Z Ingredient Guide" (page 282).

WIMPY DRINKERS A few really useful flowers and foliage have a hard time drinking immediately after harvest, but once plumped up, they make fantastic, long-lasting bouquet ingredients. For these, immediately after harvest, dip the bottom few inches of the stems into boiling water for 7 to 10 seconds (in a heat-safe container that you use only for flowers), shown top left, at which point you will notice the stems changing color and texture, or use Quick Dip, mentioned shortly; then place in cool water. This treatment works like magic for hydrating and perking up wilt-prone ingredients such as scented geranium, dusty miller, basil, honeywort, and hellebores.

WOODY BRANCHES Many shrubs and flowering trees with woody stems are great in bouquets but require a little bit of extra effort to ensure that they drink quickly. If the stems are thick, split the bottom 2 to 3 in (5 to 8 cm) of the stem ends with heavy-duty clippers, shown bottom left, then grasp one side of the sliced stem and twist it backward. Dip the ends into Quick Dip, then place immediately in a bucket of cool water that includes hydration solution if you're using it. Set the bucket in a cool, dark place for at least 6 hours before arranging.

SAP PRODUCERS Some flowers, such as euphorbia and daffodils (*Narcissus*), emit a toxic sap that can damage other flowers if not handled properly. For euphorbia, dip the stem ends into boiling water for 7 to 10 seconds to stop the flow of milky sap. Daffodils should be cut and placed in their own separate bucket and left to rest for 3 to 4 hours before mixing with other ingredients. Do not recut stems after treatment, or the sap will start oozing again. Wear long sleeves and gloves when harvesting euphorbia and daffodils, as their sap can irritate skin.

DIRTY FLOWERS A handful of garden flowers have a bad habit of turning their vase water dark and murky overnight, even with floral preservative. Black-eyed Susans, yarrow, kale, chrysanthemums, and zinnias all fall into this category. To combat this, add a few drops of bleach to the water.

Flower Life Extenders

A few items will keep your ingredients fresh while they're waiting to be arranged and looking good once they're in a bouquet.

HOLDING SOLUTION If you've harvested or bought flowers but are not going to design with them for a few days, keep them in a cool place in water mixed with holding solution. Two options I like are 200 Storage from Floralife and Professional #2 from Chrysal.

FLORAL COOLER If you're just designing for yourself, family, and friends, keeping your flowers in a cool spot after harvest is sufficient. But if you're creating arrangements as a business, a floral cooler is key, as it will allow you to store blooms much longer.

FLOWER FOOD You may wonder whether the little packets of flower food that come with most grocery store bouquets are actually beneficial. They are. Commercial flower food, also known as floral preservative, contains different formulas of three key ingredients: sugar, an acidifier, and a biocide. Combined, they work together to feed the flower, keep the environment acidic to promote water uptake, and fend off harmful bacteria.

If you're arranging flowers purely for yourself and don't want to invest in flower food, don't worry. While the use of these products definitely helps, it is not absolutely necessary and shouldn't dissuade you from enjoying your blooms. Just follow all the best practices for harvesting that I describe here and change the water in your vase every other day, and your flowers should still have a good vase life.

However, if you plan to sell your flowers or want to extend their vase life, commercial flower food is essential. These solutions have been shown to extend the vase life of cut flowers by more than 60 percent. Typical blooms that might last 5 days in untreated water will persist for 7 to 9 days if you add preservative, and the color will stay vibrant and the petals will remain plump longer.

Two popular products are Flower Food 300 from Floralife and Universal Flower Food from Chrysal. Add these to your vase water before arranging, and they will keep flowers looking good—and lasting longer. Also, if you want flowers such as peonies, garden roses, and lilies to open and color up quickly for an event, recut the stems and put them in warm water with one of these solutions.

Hydration Products

If you're buying from a wholesaler and don't know how the flowers have been cared for, or if you're simply working with flowers frequently, you'll want to add hydration products to your supplies. They can increase vase life by as much as 60 percent, and although created for professionals, they're available to everyone. They're ideal for ingredients that have a hard time taking up water, and we use them on many of the varieties we cut.

QUICK DIP As mentioned earlier, Quick Dip from Floralife is an alternative to the boiling water treatment. It jump-starts the hydration process and revives wilted blooms for some of the more finicky flowers like scented geraniums and hydrangeas. Simply dip the bottom few inches of freshly cut stems into the concentrated solution for a couple of seconds and then place in water with your desired floral preservative.

HYDRATION SOLUTION Many flowers benefit from being placed in water with hydration solution right after you buy or harvest them, especially in the heat of the summer. Leave ingredients in the solution until you're ready to design with them. Hydraflor from Floralife and OVB from Chrysal are two popular hydration products. Be sure to follow package instructions.

Design

For years, I taught intensive, hands-on floral design workshops at our farm, and I had the great pleasure of hosting hundreds of flower lovers from around the globe. At the start of every workshop, I found that most of our students shared the same struggles: they felt overwhelmed when selecting colors, weren't sure how to choose a balanced ingredient mix, didn't understand how to build arrangements, and generally lacked confidence about the whole process. But as I encouraged them to discover their own unique style and outlined my approach in clear, easy-to-follow steps, I found that by the end of the workshop these same students were creating wildly beautiful bouquets.

I aim to do the same for you by breaking down the most important elements of design so that they're easy to understand. In the previous chapter, I talked about the fundamentals of using floral mechanics and how your vase shape affects the kind of bouquet you'll build. Here, I offer additional layers of knowledge for choosing color and gathering no-fail ingredients, and I'll walk you step by step through some of the bouquet styles you'll use most.

The arrangements you'll see in this book reflect the best of what's in season, and they look like I just picked an armload of flowers from the garden—because that's exactly what I did. While tightly packed flowers in dome-shaped bouquets have their place, in my designs I aim to mimic the way plants grow in nature to show off their inherent traits. I do this by placing sprays of blooms at staggered heights, giving stems room to breathe rather than packing them too densely, and rotating the direction flowers face so that some are oriented to the side, downward, and even to the rear, since the back side of a flower is often just as beautiful, and sometimes more nuanced, than the front. And that's what you'll learn to do, too.

Design Fundamentals

Along with the specific arrangement instructions I will detail shortly, these tips will help you create the most beautiful bouquets possible.

CONSIDER THE VIEWPOINT

Before you begin, think about where you'll place your finished bouquet, and how people will view and interact with it. Will it sit on a mantel where only the front will be seen, flank a doorway with flowers at eye level, or serve as a dining table centerpiece that's enjoyed from all sides? This will help you determine where and how you'll place your flowers. I set a lazy Susan on top of an upside-down bucket and then rotate as I add ingredients. When making bouquets that will be viewed from multiple angles, a lazy Susan is a fantastic tool that allows you to turn and view as you're arranging.

MODIFY INGREDIENTS

Often you'll come across a beautiful ingredient with an element that doesn't complement your arrangement, such as a fruited branch with too many leaves or a foliage plant with flowers that don't support your color palette. You can easily remedy this by snipping out the parts you don't want in order to highlight what is most important and will enhance the final arrangement. I regularly remove foliage from fruiting branches so that the fruit is more visible and snip the glaring yellow flowers from senecio, one of my favorite silver foliage plants.

PAY ATTENTION TO PROPORTIONS

A good rule is to keep your ingredient height one to two times the height of your vase. For example, if I'm using a vessel that's 1 ft (30 cm) tall, I'll keep my flowers and foliage between 1 and 2 ft (30 to 61 cm) beyond the vessel, for a total height (including the vase) between 2 and 3 ft (61 and 91 cm). If your ingredients are shorter, they'll look unsubstantial; if they're taller, they may look out of proportion and become unstable.

WORK AROUND THE PERIMETER

Begin by adding ingredients around the outside edge of your vessel, slowly layering as you work your way in. This leaves room in the center for your showiest flowers.

PACE YOURSELF

It can be easy to hyper focus or to panic and frantically add to your arrangement. My advice is to slow down, and if you're feeling rushed or anxious, take a breath, step back, and look at the arrangement with some perspective. Work intentionally, following each step outlined in the "Essential Techniques" (page 68), one at a time, rather than bouncing back and forth from step to step. Give yourself space to consider how everything is working together, and make adjustments as necessary.

KNOW WHEN TO STOP

One of the most commonly asked questions is: How will I know when I'm done with a bouquet? To achieve the natural-looking styles shown here, the goal is for your arrangement to be full and lush but not so jam-packed that ingredients compete for space. It's easy to keep adding simply because you have flowers left, but do so only if they fill a need. Otherwise, your finished arrangement may end up looking stuffed and tight. The more you practice, the better you'll be able to tell when you're finished. And if you overdo it, you can always remove material.

HONE YOUR SKILLS

The most important thing you can do to become an expert arranger is to practice as much as you possibly can. When you first start making bouquets, you'll find yourself hesitating between steps, questioning the placement of each flower, focusing too much on one particular element, and driving yourself a little crazy in the process. But if you keep at it and continue to experiment, you'll discover that the process becomes more fluid and natural with every bouquet that you make, eventually becoming second nature.

Understanding Color

Color preferences are extremely personal, and what appeals to one person might not to someone else. How you use color in everyday life, and in your bouquets, can be one of the most beautiful forms of self-expression, so it's helpful to understand how colors work together so you can achieve the results you're aiming for.

If you read the countless articles available on color theory and the science behind color, it's easy to feel overwhelmed by all the technical terms that don't necessarily translate to the natural world. And many of the hues in arrangements—including chocolate, copper, and silver, all of which I commonly use—aren't even represented on the color wheel. So when you approach color in terms of floral ingredients, here are a few concepts to keep in mind.

WARM VERSUS COOL

After years of teaching, what I find most useful is to understand the difference between warm and cool tones. Every color on the spectrum has warm and cool versions. Even color categories that we typically think of as warm—yellow, orange, and red—have cool shades within them. Likewise, color categories thought of as cool—purple, blue, and green—have warm shades.

For example, when it comes to roses, peonies, and dahlias, there are hundreds of different pink varieties available, and each one leans toward

being warm or cool. Pink with even the tiniest bit of yellow is warm, with colors ranging from light to dark in blush, peach, raspberry, coral, and cherry. If you instead add even a small hint of blue to pink, you'll find cool tones in shell pink, rose, magenta, scarlet, and blood red.

Unless you're deliberately trying to create contrast, in general you'll build the most appealing bouquets when you use ingredients that are either all warm tones or all cool tones. Understanding this will help you assemble a gorgeous color palette every time.

SHADES OF GREEN

Foliage creates the base of every arrangement I make and also adds dimension and texture. Many people think that flowers are the most important element of a beautiful arrangement, but in my experience, having a vast selection of leaves, vines, and textural pods is what really sets seasonally inspired arrangements apart because, as you move through the year, you'll have access to much more interesting material than with standard imported foliage options. The choices of greens are limitless, and keep in mind that they,

too, cover a spectrum of warm and cool tones. On the cool side, there's rich emerald, forest green, silver, and gray. On the warm side, there's grass green, apple green, and brilliant chartreuse. I typically don't like to combine warm-toned and cool-toned foliage—such as lime and silver—in the same arrangement, since their contrast can be harsh. Once you pick warm or cool greens for a bouquet, stay within those tones for all of your foliage ingredients.

COLOR FROM FOLIAGE

Once you start working with what's seasonally available, you'll become more aware of all the colors found in nature. Beyond green, leaves—as well as buds, seedpods, berries, and grassy seed heads—come in their own spectrum of hues, including gold, copper, crimson, plum, frosty blue, gunmetal, and even black.

Over the course of the growing season, most plants will go through great changes, and their leaves, pods, and blossoms will transform before your eyes—all of which increase the ways you

can use them in arrangements. For example, in spring, the arching stems of ninebark are covered in bright cranberry buds that give way to an explosion of delicate creamy blooms. The flowers are short-lived, and as soon as their petals drop, they leave behind exquisite seedpods that darken as they age. These subtle color changes make for the most magical ingredients.

LAYERING

With so many beautiful choices in any given season, it's easy to become overly enthusiastic and combine too many colors in an arrangement. While a rainbow is beautiful in its own right, for flower arranging it's important to give the eye somewhere to rest—and that can be difficult when you incorporate more than a few hues. When making a bouquet, I highly recommend that you narrow your choices and feature one or two main tones, then layer your ingredients from there. Layering is achieved by selecting flowers and foliage

in a particular color range and using only shades within that range. This allows you to explore and highlight the nuanced details in buds, veining, seedpods, and variegation. As a result, your finished arrangement will have a cohesive and harmonious quality. For example, when working with yellow, you can vary the levels of saturation by choosing a wide palette of ingredients in that tone to add depth and dimension. If you're new to flower arranging or want guaranteed success, pick one color and layer within it.

COLOR BRIDGING

Once you master the art of layering, the next skill to learn is color bridging: the process of marrying two colors that are further apart on the spectrum. You start with the two tones that you want to combine, selecting a range of material in each so that you have multiple layers to work with. Then you find ingredients that contain both of the hues—these are called bridges. For example, to combine soft blush garden roses with deep maroon cosmos and dark foliage, you can use trumpet lilies that have a light inner throat and deep outer veining

to tie the light and dark tones together. You'll find great bridges by paying close attention to subtle details such as streaking, veining, and the gentle cast of a different hue on the back of leaves or petals. When you're pulling together ingredients for an arrangement that includes two or more colors that seem far apart, use plenty of bridging material, so your arrangement doesn't end up having a polka-dot quality and nowhere for the eye to rest.

Fundamental Ingredients

I'm passionate about creating bouquets that have a lush, abundant look and show off each ingredient's most beautiful, natural features, like arching stems, frilly foliage, and giant blooms in rich hues. I can't overemphasize how important it is to seek out the best local, seasonally available flowers and foliage you can find; their diversity, and their inherent freshness and features, are what will make your arrangements stop people in their tracks.

To create this style of bouquet, it's essential to gather material from each of the six fundamental ingredient categories highlighted in the pages ahead. The first three—*structural foliage*, *supporting ingredient*, and *textural ingredient*—form the base of a bouquet. The next three—*supporting flowers*, *focal flowers*, and *airy accents*—provide all the intricate, eye-catching details. Each ingredient serves a specific purpose, and if you include all of them, your finished displays will be stunning.

Many plants' features change throughout the year, so it's useful to note that some ingredients can serve as multiple types depending on what part of the plant you're highlighting, how they're used among the other flowers and foliage in an arrangement, and the proportions of the finished bouquet. For example, in winter, when focal flower options are more limited, a tulip could be a focal flower, whereas in spring it's often a supporting flower. A pansy could be the supporting flower if larger focals are in the mix, or it could be the focal flower in a smaller display. Hellebores can be focal or supporting flowers depending on what they're combined with, or even textural ingredients if you're using their seedpods.

It's not important to think of given materials as always serving the same function; instead, include a flower or foliage option that fills each category so that you'll end up with a balanced arrangement. For most of the projects in this book, ingredients are added in the order in which they're listed. I look at each category as a step, and I often use more than one kind of any given ingredient type in my bouquets. The wider the variety, the more interesting the result will be. I show some of my favorite ingredient options in the pages ahead, though many more choices are available.

Structural Foliage

As the name implies, structural foliage establishes the framework and ultimate size of an arrangement. It forms the shape on which every successive ingredient is layered. This category is filled with cuttings from shrubs, trees, and woody branches.

Blueberry

Raspberry

Tatarian honeysuckle

Ninebark

Viburnum

Mock orange

Ninebark

European hornbeam

Crabapple

Beech

Viburnum

Vine maple

56

SUMMER STRUCTURAL FOLIAGE

Raspberry

Ninebark

European hornbeam

Privet

Crabapple

Beech

WINTER STRUCTURAL FOLIAGE

Rockrose

Holly

Evergreens

Boxwood

Laurel

Eleagnus

DESIGN

Supporting Ingredients

After you establish an arrangement's shape using structural foliage, supporting ingredients (which are typically a bit shorter than structural foliage) mimic the existing framework and create a nest for the next ingredients. This category is vast and can contain just about any foliage plant. Some of my favorites are mint, bells of Ireland, and lady's mantle.

SPRING SUPPORTING INGREDIENTS

Mint

Spirea

Solomon's seal

Lady's mantle

Rockrose

Honeywort

AUTUMN SUPPORTING INGREDIENTS

Viburnum

Smokebush

Hydrangea

Apple of Peru

Hypericum

Amaranth

58

Scented geranium

Bells of Ireland

Artemisia

Oregano

Basil

Bupleurum

59

Euphorbia

Rosemary

Ivy

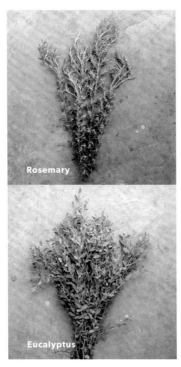

Boxwood

Eucalyptus

Scented geranium

Textural Ingredients

After supporting ingredients are in place, textural ingredients help add dimension and movement to an arrangement. This category often includes foliage with a curving or weeping habit, vines, fruit on the branch, berries, pods, and ferns.

Akebia

Honeysuckle

Angelica

Goat's beard

Clematis

Sweet pea

Rose hips

Porcelain berry

Pokeweed

Hops

Blackberry

Bittersweet

60

SUMMER TEXTURAL INGREDIENTS

Cress

Passion vine

Love-in-a-mist

Nasturtium

Love-in-a-puff vine

Pea vine

61

WINTER TEXTURAL INGREDIENTS

Fern

Nandina

Filbert

Pieris

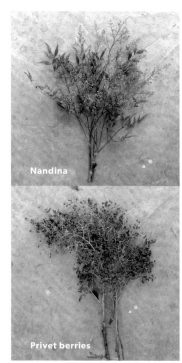

Privet berries

Martagon lily pods

Supporting Flowers

Once you've created your base with the first three fundamental ingredients, supporting flowers infuse bouquets with color and interest. They're typically stems with sprays of blossoms, but if these aren't available, it's important to add blooms in clusters or multiples to mimic how they grow naturally in the garden. This category includes Iceland poppies, small-flowered zinnias, cosmos, and pincushion flowers.

Narcissus

Foxglove

Larkspur

Sweet pea

Calendula

Canterbury bells

Nasturtium

Tickseed

Marigold

Gomphrena

Chrysanthemum

Japanese anemone

62

SUMMER SUPPORTING FLOWERS

Cosmos

Zinnia

Rose

Yarrow

Strawflower

Echinacea

WINTER SUPPORTING FLOWERS

Hellebore

Anemone

Ranunculus

Iceland poppy

Kale (flowering)

Narcissus

Focal Flowers

Focal flowers are the featured blooms that are supported and highlighted by all of the other ingredients. They're typically larger, showier flowers such as peonies, garden roses, and dahlias. Each season has its floral stars, and I like to build each bouquet around one of those stars.

Anemone

Narcissus

Tulip

Ranunculus

Rose

Iceland poppy

Zinnia

Marigold

China aster

Black-eyed Susan

Dahlia

Chrysanthemum

Peony

Rose

Zinnia

Cosmos

Lily

Dahlia

Ranunculus

Amaryllis

Iceland poppy

Kale (flowering)

Poinsettia

Tulip

Airy Accents

Too frequently overlooked, airy accents are the ingredients that add magic to an arrangement. These delicate details are the finishing touches that take a bouquet to the next level, catching people's attention from across the room and drawing them in. These include materials like feathery grasses, shimmering pods that sparkle in the slightest breeze, and tiny ethereal flowers.

SPRING AIRY ACCENTS

AUTUMN AIRY ACCENTS

Columbine

Fritillaria

Heuchera

Blue bells

Leucojum

Bleeding heart

Feverfew

Grass

Flowering tobacco

Grain

Black-eyed Susan

Snowberry

Campion

Martagon lily

Forget-me-not

False Queen Anne's lace

Mignonette

Sea holly

Nandina

Pepper tree

Cress

Grass

Clematis seed heads

Birch catkins

Essential Techniques

(1) Compress a piece of chicken wire into a ball and push it down into the vase. Secure the chicken wire by making an X across the top with waterproof tape. Fill the vase almost to the brim with water.

(2) Establish the shape and ultimate size of the arrangement by placing the structural foliage around the perimeter of the vase. It should essentially form three points of a triangle with uneven sides, with the highest point in the back left or right, a midpoint on the other rear side, and the lowest point spilling over the front edge. Stair-stepping the three points creates a natural, sweeping look with interest and movement, and all the other elements will fill in between and around this framework. This also balances the ingredients' weight, which is essential when building any large arrangement. Here, Tatarian honeysuckle establishes the highest point in the back left, the midpoint to the right, and the third point on the front left.

(3) Insert the supporting ingredient, mimicking the same triangle. Use pieces that are slightly shorter than your structural foliage, and fill in gaps to give the bouquet a lush look. I've used *Rosa dupontii* because its slightly nodding flowers give the arrangement an ethereal feel and convey a cascading abundance.

(4) Add the textural ingredient, again repeating the same shape, and weaving it between the other ingredients to add movement and color. I used *Deutzia scabra* 'Codsall Pink' because its beautiful pastel sprays add a cloud-like quality and punctuate all the green.

continued

73

(5) Insert the first of the supporting flowers in gaps left by the other elements. Here, the towering, snaking stems of pale peach 'Sutton's Apricot' foxglove add height and reach to the fluffy arrangement.

(6) Your focal flowers are always the stars of your arrangement; everything else is there to support them. Add them toward the end so you can make sure to give them prime visibility. Place them throughout, starting in the center and working your way out. Give each bloom room to breathe, and cut stems as needed so that they're at varying heights. I chose four pale pink peony varieties with different flower shapes to add even more interest.

(7) Intersperse the remaining supporting flowers. 'Adélaïde d'Orléans' roses woven throughout, especially between the larger focal blooms, tie the whole bouquet together with color and movement.

(8) Tuck in the delicate airy accents. I used the last three stems of 'Pink Morning' martagon lilies from our fields and a bundle of sanguisorba 'Pink Elephant' that looks like miniature fireworks.

75

Essential Technique: Centerpiece

Centerpieces are perfect for dressing up a coffee or dining table. For this type of arrangement, I love using a footed vessel, so I can feature ingredients that want to tumble over the edge, like vines and fruit on the branch. Choose a vessel with a flared rim, at least 4 in (10 cm) deep, to hold sufficient water and support stems. Be sure to add ingredients at a horizontal angle to keep the shape low and wide, especially if it's going to be placed on a dining table, so you don't block anyone's view while they're sitting. Good mechanics (see page 21) are essential to achieving this look.

When assembling a centerpiece, you'll want to elevate your vase using a lazy Susan on top of an upside-down bucket, and rotating as you work to view all sides. As for placing your blooms, the exact order in which you add your focal and supporting flowers is less important than making sure your focal flowers are the most prominent ingredients in your bouquet and they're placed in a way that shows them off.

INGREDIENTS

STRUCTURAL FOLIAGE
Raspberry 'Tulameen'
6 stems, 8 to 12 in (20 to 30 cm) long

SUPPORTING INGREDIENT
Blueberry 'Duke' foliage and unripe fruit
7 stems, 10 to 12 in (25 to 30 cm) long

TEXTURAL INGREDIENTS
Honeysuckle 'Scentsation' foliage with flowers
8 stems, 6 to 12 in (15 to 30 cm) long

Goat's beard
7 stems, 10 in (25 cm) long

SUPPORTING FLOWERS
Rose 'Malvern Hills'
6 sprays, 8 in (20 cm) long

California poppy 'Milkmaid'
12 stems, 8 to 12 in (20 to 30 cm) long

FOCAL FLOWER
Rose 'The Pilgrim'
11 stems, 8 to 10 in (20 to 25 cm) long

AIRY ACCENT
Mexican feather grass (*Stipa tenuissima*)
15 stems, 12 to 15 in (30 to 38 cm) long

VASE: Object & Totem

(1)

(2)

(3)

(4)

(1) Compress a piece of chicken wire into a ball and push it down into a vase that has a flower frog in place. Secure the chicken wire by making an X across the top with waterproof tape. Fill the vase almost to the brim with water.

(2) You will be building from the outside in. Establish the shape and ultimate size of the arrangement by placing the structural foliage around the perimeter of the vase. It should essentially form three points of a triangle with uneven sides, setting the highest point in the back left or right, a midpoint on the other rear side, and the lowest point spilling over the front edge. Stair-stepping the three points creates a natural, sweeping look with interest and movement, and all the other elements fill in between and around this framework. This also distributes weight, which is critical when creating any large display. Raspberry canes have a great natural arch, and we have so much growing on our farm that we use it a lot. Whatever grows abundantly in your garden may be a great structural option.

(3) Insert the supporting ingredient. Echo the triangle, extending the pieces outward horizontally. It's important to keep this type of arrangement low and wide rather than tall and skinny, because it is typically viewed on a table, and you don't want diners' views of each other to be blocked. Insert the stems at an angle so they cascade over the lip of the vessel and spill over the side. Blueberry foliage with immature fruit provides a textural quality and adds dimension.

(4) Tuck in the first textural ingredient, echoing the points of the triangle, and using varying lengths to create movement and variety. 'Scentsation' honeysuckle foliage and flowers add a bit of wildness.

continued

79

(5)

(6)

(7)

(8)

(5) Add the focal flowers, echoing the arrangement's arching shape, and staggering the flowers to create a layered effect. 'The Pilgrim' roses' clusters of big, pillowy blooms add an additional layer of complexity.

(6) Thread in the second textural ingredient, goat's beard, among the larger flowers. While it's technically a flower, if picked before fully opened it has a very textural quality.

(7) Add the supporting flowers throughout the arrangement. Here I've used 'Malvern Hills' spray rose and California poppy 'Milkmaid' because both have delicate miniature flowers that add dimension and color.

(8) Tuck in the airy accent. The golden seed heads of *Stipa tenuissima* add sparkle to the arrangement when touched by even the slightest breeze.

81

Essential Technique: Vignette

A vignette is a simple way of making a big impact with a small quantity of flowers, and it's also a great way to highlight one type of flower on a smaller scale than you would with the en masse technique. When displaying a vignette of flowers, you can either make mini bouquets with multiple ingredients in each vessel, or keep it simple and fill vases with just one variety of flower. Displaying blooms in this way is ideal for a long, narrow setting: think windowsill, mantel, or table. I keep a collection of small vessels in varied shapes, sizes, and heights just to create vignettes.

INGREDIENTS (ALL FOCAL FLOWERS)

Rose 'Grace'
12 stems, 7 to 12 in (18 to 30 cm) long

Rose 'Carding Mill'
5 stems, 12 to 20 in (30 to 51 cm) long and
10 stems, 5 to 8 in (13 to 20 cm) long

Rose 'Lady of Shalott'
11 stems, 6 to 14 in (15 to 36 cm) long

Rose 'The Lark Ascending'
8 stems, 7 to 10 in (18 to 25 cm) long

Rose 'Port Sunlight'
7 stems, 5 to 7 in (13 to 18 cm) long

Rose 'Ambridge Rose'
2 stems, 5 to 7 in (13 to 18 cm) long

Rose 'Colette'
2 stems, 5 in (13 cm) long

Rose 'Wollerton Old Hall'
7 stems, 5 to 8 in (13 to 20 cm) long

Rose 'Comtes de Champagne'
5 stems, 5 to 9 in (13 to 23 cm) long

(1)

(2)

(3)

(4)

(1) Fill a collection of small bottles and/ or vases with water. I like to choose a wide variety of sizes and shapes. Pitchers, jars, and bud vases are all good candidates.

(2) Working around the perimeter in the larger vessels, add a base layer of flowers so that they look like they are spilling over the edges.

(3) Cut longer stems and thread them in on top of the first layer for height and dimension.

(4) In the remaining vessels, add individual stems of varieties you want to feature. Group all the vases into a display.

Essential Technique: Posy

A posy is a petite arrangement, ideal for featuring shorter-stemmed ingredients or treasured varieties that would get lost in bigger bouquets. The exact order in which you add your focal and supporting flowers is less important than making sure your focal flowers are the most prominent ingredients in your bouquet and they're placed in a way that shows them off. Posies don't have to be ornate or elaborate, and they are right at home on a bedside or kitchen table. Since they're a perfect size to give as a gift, I recommend keeping a stock of inexpensive vases on hand so you can give a posy on short notice. Rather than using jars whose openings are narrower than their bases—which would force the flowers upright, creating a stiffer finished look—find vases with more flared openings, similar in shape to a pint glass, which lend themselves to natural-looking arrangements. The result will feel much more loose and abundant.

INGREDIENTS

STRUCTURAL FOLIAGE
Raspberry 'Tulameen'
4 stems, 8 to 12 in (20 to 30 cm) long

SUPPORTING INGREDIENT
Ninebark stems with seedcases
6 branching stems, 6 to 12 in (15 to 30 cm) long

TEXTURAL INGREDIENTS
Raspberry 'Tulameen'
4 stems, 8 to 14 in (20 to 36 cm) long, leaves removed

Salvia 'Ember's Wish'
4 stems, 10 to 14 in (25 to 36 cm) long

SUPPORTING FLOWERS
Zinnia 'Queen Lime Blush'
2 stems, 8 to 12 in (20 to 30 cm) long

Echinacea Supreme 'Flamingo'
2 stems, 8 to 12 in (20 to 30 cm) long

FOCAL FLOWERS
Rose 'Benjamin Britten'
5 stems, 6 to 12 in (15 to 30 cm) long

Rose 'Boscobel'
4 stems, 6 to 12 in (15 to 30 cm) long

AIRY ACCENT
Sanguisorba 'Pink Elephant'
4 stems, 8 to 12 in (20 to 30 cm) long

VASE: Farmhouse Pottery

(1)

(2)

(3)

(4)

(1) Secure a flower frog in the bottom of the vase. You can also use a ball of chicken wire for extra support. Fill the vase almost to the brim with water.

(2) Establish the shape and ultimate size of the arrangement by placing the structural foliage around the perimeter of the vase at varying heights. As you work, make sure to secure stems into the flower frog for stability. For a simple posy, it's important to make a nest of foliage that will support all the other ingredients. Here I've used raspberry foliage with the fruit attached.

(3) Place the supporting ingredient, at varying heights, in the pockets left by the structural foliage. I used stems of ninebark seed cases, with all of the foliage removed, for color and to carry a coppery hue throughout.

(4) Insert the first textural ingredient. More raspberries, this time with all of the leaves removed, highlight the fruit and add a pop of red to the arrangement's base.

continued

(5)

(6)

(7)

(8)

(5) Add the second textural ingredient. Salvia brings in additional color and dimension, with vertical spires that carry the shape of the vase up into the arrangement.

(6) Place large focal flowers throughout, starting in the center and working your way outward. As needed, cut stems at varying heights so the bouquet doesn't look too domed. I used a mix of 'Benjamin Britten' and 'Boscobel' roses.

(7) Thread in the smaller supporting flowers, making sure to scatter them in between the larger blooms and add color to any dark spots.

(8) Tuck in the airy accent. Sanguisorba adds movement and sparkle.

91

Essential Technique: Hand-Tied Market Bouquet

This technique is one that you'll use often because you can mix whatever ingredients you have on hand and put it together quickly and easily. It's perfect for gifting. Unlike an arrangement in a vase, where you see the sides of the bouquet, for a market bouquet you want to position the blooms on the top part of the arrangement because the paper wrap will hide the edges. The fundamental ingredient types aren't significant in terms of the order in which you'll add them, but thinking about the different types when gathering your flowers and foliage will result in a good overall mix.

INGREDIENTS

STRUCTURAL FOLIAGE

Common privet
2 stems, 24 in (61 cm) long

Mock orange (*Philadelphus*)
3 stems, 24 in (61 cm) long

SUPPORTING INGREDIENTS

Pineapple mint
3 stems, 20 in (51 cm) long

Dock (*Rumex crispus*)
5 stems, 24 in (61 cm) long

TEXTURAL INGREDIENT

Oats (*Avena sativa*)
5 stems, 24 in (61 cm) long

SUPPORTING FLOWERS

Foxglove 'Alba'
5 stems, 24 in (61 cm) long

Feverfew 'Tetra White Wonder'
5 stems, 20 to 24 in (51 to 61 cm) long

FOCAL FLOWER

Peony 'Marie Lemoine'
5 stems, 20 in (51 cm) long

AIRY ACCENT

Sweet pea 'White Frills'
7 stems, 18 in (46 cm) long

WRAPPING SUPPLIES

2 by 2 ft (60 by 60 cm) square of kraft paper

Flower "diaper" made of Eco Fresh Bouquet stem wrap or paper towel, soaked in water

Plastic bag

2 rubber bands

30 in (76 cm) natural twine or ribbon

(1)

(2)

(3)

(4)

(1) Before beginning, prep ingredients by removing one-half to two-thirds of the lower foliage from stems. On your work surface, lay the flowers in piles by variety with the heads facing away from you. Set aside any delicate or airy accents that you want to highlight; you'll add these near the end.

(2) To begin the arrangement, choose an upright focal flower with a long sturdy stem for the center. Add a few stems of structural foliage and supporting flowers around both sides of the starting focal flower. I used privet and feverfew.

(3) Add ingredients so that they're at a roughly 25-degree angle to the starting stem. (A few stems were removed from this photo to clearly show the angle at which you want to add ingredients.) The order in which you add the remaining flowers and foliage doesn't matter, as long as you focus on evenly distributing them throughout in a way that looks good to your eye.

(4) Continue adding ingredients at an angle, and twist the bouquet after every few additions. I generally work in a clockwise direction, adding a few stems at a 25-degree angle with my right hand. Then I twist the bouquet slightly with my left hand before adding the next ingredients. You can go either clockwise or counterclockwise; just be consistent, or your stems will end up in a tangled mess.

continued

(5) Once your bouquet is as big as you want it, look for any gaps in the arrangement. Lift any ingredients that have sunk below the surface, and thread in additional stems and airy accents.

(6) Trim the stem ends to your desired length with a pair of sharp snips. I cut everything to about 18 in (46 cm).

(7) Secure the stem ends with a rubber band. Holding the bouquet with one hand, slip a rubber band around one or two strong stems, about a third of the way up the stem handle.

(8) Continue holding the bouquet with one hand and wrap the rubber band around the stems two times, winding down toward the cut ends. Once you've reached the bottom, slip the rubber band end around another woody stem to secure. This technique allows you to easily release the rubber band and adjust the bouquet if needed, then resecure the stem ends quickly. Keep the stems in water until you're ready to wrap.

continued

97

(9)

(10)

(11)

(12)

(9) Lay the kraft paper on a table. Cover the stem ends with wet stem wrap or paper towel, cover tightly with the plastic bag, and secure the bag with a rubber band. Then lay the bouquet diagonally on the paper.

(10) Fold the bottom corner of the paper up and over the stem wrap and crease it down so it stays in place.

(11) Pull one side of the paper around the front of the bouquet, then pull the other corner over the first so that they slightly overlap.

(12) Secure in place with twine or ribbon.

Essential Technique: Bridal Bouquet

Once your family and friends find out you arrange flowers, you'll surely be asked to create a bridal bouquet. The technique is much like a market bouquet but with two important differences. First, for a bridal bouquet, you want to select ingredients that are more wilt proof. Those with woody stems, such as ninebark, roses, and viburnum, are ideal because the bouquet will be out of water for an extended period. Second, it's essential to remove foliage from 80 percent of each stem, leaving just 2 to 3 in (5 to 7.5 cm) of flowers and foliage at the very top. If too much material remains on the stem, the finished bouquet will be very bulky and heavy. As with a market bouquet, the order in which you'll add the fundamental ingredient types isn't significant; just keep thinking about the different types when gathering your flowers and foliage, and you'll achieve a good overall mix.

INGREDIENTS

STRUCTURAL FOLIAGE
Ninebark 'Diablo'
8 stems, 18 in (46 cm) long

Viburnum 'Popcorn' foliage
12 stems, 18 in (46 cm) long

SUPPORTING INGREDIENTS
Smokebush 'Grace'
5 stems, 18 in (46 cm) long

PeeGee hydrangea 'Unique'
with unripe flowers
8 stems, 18 in (46 cm) long

TEXTURAL INGREDIENTS
Autumn fern
3 stems, 18 in (46 cm) long

Goat's beard
5 stems, 18 in (46 cm) long

Raspberry 'Tulameen', unripe fruit
8 stems, 18 in (46 cm) long

Heuchera 'Green Spice'
3 stems, 18 in (46 cm) long

SUPPORTING FLOWERS
Rose 'Sally Holmes'
4 stems, 18 in (46 cm) long

Spray rose 'Penelope'
3 stems, 18 in (46 cm) long

FOCAL FLOWERS
Ranunculus 'La Belle Champagne'
2 stems, 18 in (46 cm) long

Rose 'Abraham Darby'
9 stems, 18 in (46 cm) long

AIRY ACCENT
Sweet pea 'Mollie Rilstone'
5 stems, 18 in (46 cm) long

RIBBON SUPPLIES
Oasis waterproof tape or twine

5 yd (4.5 m) ribbon

Pin (I use 1½ in [4 cm] boutonniere pins—straight pins with decorative heads)

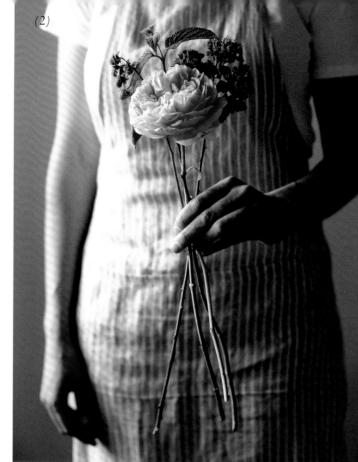

(5) Look for gaps in the arrangement. Lift any ingredients that have dropped below the surface, and thread in additional ingredients and airy accents.

(6) To give the bouquet a beautiful finished look, tuck sturdy, wilt-proof foliage—I used viburnum and ninebark; senecio is also a good choice—into any empty spots around the outside, essentially forming a loose collar around the outer edge.

(7) Trim the stem ends with a pair of sharp snips so they are all the same length. I cut everything down to 12 in (30 cm).

(8) Secure the flowers in place with Oasis waterproof tape or twine. I prefer using tape because it guarantees that the stems will stay right where I placed them. For a looser, fuller look, tape no more than 1 to 2 in (3 to 5 cm) of the handle stem bundle length, right near the collar. Leave the stems in water until it's time to finish the bouquet with your choice of ribbon.

continued

(9)

(10)

(11)

(12)

(9) Hold one end of the ribbon against the stem handle with one finger, and use your other hand to wrap the ribbon around the handle.

(10) Wrap the ribbon snugly around the handle at least twice at the starting point, then pull to tighten. Continue wrapping as you wind the ribbon toward the top of the handle, making sure to cover the edge of each ribbon wrapping as you go. I wrap the ribbon over the tape so it covers 2 to 3 in (5 to 7.5 cm) of the stems.

(11) Once you reach the top, choose the front of the bouquet. This is where you will secure the ribbon. Twist the ribbon tightly and insert a pin through the center of the twist, making sure to angle your pin down into the stems so it doesn't poke out the other side. Cut the ribbon, leaving a tail at least 3 ft (1 m) long.

(12) Lay the bouquet on a table and take another long length of ribbon (at least 2 yd [2 m]). Slip the center point under the stems and adjust it by matching up the free ends so the lengths are equal.

continued

107

(13)

(14)

(15)

(16)

(13) Tie the two ribbon lengths in a single knot close to the top of the ribbon collar.

(14) Cinch the ribbon down tight, making sure to cover the pinhead, then tie another knot to keep the ribbon in place.

(15) Use sharp scissors to trim the ends of all three ribbons at varying lengths at an angle.

(16) Hold up your bouquet to make sure none of the ribbons will trail on the ground when carried. (Note: If you're using silk ribbon, wait until the morning of the event to add it, since it can wick up moisture overnight, leaving the tails wet and floppy.)

Essential Technique: En Masse

Some flowers are so gorgeous that they deserve to be shown off all by themselves. So whenever I find myself with an abundance of a certain bloom that I want to display prominently, or I don't have the time or energy to make a more complex arrangement, I love to feature them en masse. With this technique, I rarely use any additional ingredients, but when I do I'm not concerned about adding them in a specific order. Instead, I simply use other ingredients, as needed, to highlight the main focal flower.

If you're using larger flowers, it's important to choose a heavy-bottomed container that can handle the mass and weight of the ingredients without tipping over.

INGREDIENTS (ALL FOCAL FLOWERS)

Peony 'Kansas'
7 stems/sprays, 20 to 24 in
(51 to 61 cm) long

Peony 'Edulis Superba'
4 stems, 20 to 24 in (51 to
61 cm) long

Peony 'Feather Top'
5 stems, 20 to 24 in (51 to
61 cm) long

Peony 'Monsieur Jules Elie'
5 stems, 20 to 24 in (51 to
61 cm) long

Peony 'Sea Shell'
10 stems/sprays, 20 to 24 in
(51 to 61 cm) long

Peony 'Sarah Bernhardt'
5 stems/sprays, 20 to 24 in
(51 to 61 cm) long

VASE: Farmhouse Pottery

(*1*) Compress a piece of chicken wire into a ball and push it down into the vase. Secure the chicken wire by making an *X* across the top with waterproof tape. Fill the vase to the brim with water.

(*2*) Working around the perimeter of the vase, place a base layer of flowers at an angle so they look like they are spilling over the edges. I started with the darkest of the peonies, 'Kansas', because I wanted them to have the least presence in the finished arrangement.

(*3*) Use slightly longer stems than the first to add another layer of blooms, making sure to fill in any holes. I chose rose pink peonies—'Edulis Superba', 'Feather Top', and 'Monsieur Jules Elie'—for this layer to form a fluffy pink cloud.

(*4*) Add the final layer of flowers, leaving these stems slightly longer than the first two layers. I like to save the most special and unusual varieties for the end so they are featured front and center. I chose 'Sea Shell', a beautiful single variety, and 'Sarah Bernhardt', a small candy-pink type with fluffy centers.

113

Seasonal
Bouquet

Each season offers a lush palette of plants that capture a specific moment in time. Earliest spring brings with it our first blooms, which build up to an intoxicating abundance of flowers by midsummer. As autumn comes along, we find more pods, grassy seed heads, and textural treasures. By winter, we're making the most of what's left, including rose hips, berried branches, and a handful of cold-weather blooms.

The designs that follow are based on what we can grow and gather in our local area in a given time of year. The flowers, foliage, and textural material where you live may be very different, and you'll of course have your own color preferences. Rather than trying to recreate them exactly, I suggest using these as inspiration for your own unique displays. We show all the ingredients laid out to give you a close-up view of the colors, textures, and forms, so if you like them, you can find local substitutes that are just as beautiful. Then, follow the steps previously outlined in "Essential Techniques" for the appropriate bouquet styles to celebrate the best of your region's ingredients in each season.

Spring

Of all the seasons, spring is by far my favorite because it is filled with so much hope and anticipation for the future. After a long dreary winter, it's always a thrill to watch life return to the garden and to once again begin filling my house with flowers.

In early spring, even the smallest bloom is cause for celebration. I walk the fields daily, keeping my gaze low to the ground, looking closely for signs of new growth pushing up through the soil. Narcissus are always the first to arrive, and their sweetly scented blooms are a welcome treat. As the daffodils fade, tulips take center stage and offer the first rainbow of color for the year.

All around our property, the apple, cherry, hawthorn, and plum trees start exploding into clouds of tiny pastel blooms. The bees arrive right on cue and make quick work of pollinating the trees, and on sunny days the air is filled with a light fragrance along with the sound of thousands of tiny workers buzzing away. Soon after, the blossoms give way to young fruit, and the once-bare branches are cloaked in a new set of leaves. In the hedgerows lining our field, wild roses start to flower just as the peonies and earliest perennials arrive.

As the weather warms, my neighbors emerge from their winter hibernation and can be spotted puttering around their gardens. Weekends are filled with the loud hum of lawn mowers and lots of fence-side chatting about the weather and plants. In the fields surrounding our rural neighborhood, tractors prepare the soil for planting, and farm crews return to work for the season.

Each morning the sun rises a little earlier, and the birdsongs get so loud that I can't sleep past 5 a.m. if we've left the windows open. I'm always amazed by how much changes over the course of this season: in just three short months, our previously barren landscape transforms into a dense and richly layered sea of green. And while in early spring I have to hunt for even the tiniest treasures, by the end there's more abundance and beauty pouring out of the garden than I can possibly keep up with.

Shades of Green Statement Piece

When everything is actively growing and pushing out new foliage in spring, our farm is awash in bright, glowing greens. And once the shrubs and trees around the property have leafed out, I can dive into flower arranging in earnest.

One of my very favorite early-blooming shrubs to work with is viburnum. There are so many different varieties: some have white lacy flowers, others have chartreuse blooms that mature to white, and others are grown primarily for their brilliantly colored fruit. My favorite variety of all is 'Popcorn', which I learned about from my first flower friend, Nina, who lived just down the road. Nina had an established 'Popcorn' viburnum that she always cut from to make birthday party arrangements for my daughter, Elora. One year, she generously made flower crowns with puffs of viburnum and lilacs for all the girls and their American Girl dolls. Each spring, when this treasured variety bursts into bloom, I think of Nina.

Early in the season, when little is in bloom, I love making monochromatic bouquets that celebrate what's growing in the garden, and a crisp white-and-Granny-Smith-apple-green pairing is always a sure bet. This bouquet was inspired by Nina's viburnum. In my favorite Frances Palmer vase, billowy viburnum blooms team up with creamy daffodils (*Narcissus*), 'Green Star' tulips, and hellebores that look like shooting stars. Wild heuchera brings a delicate, ethereal quality to the arrangement.

INGREDIENTS

Structural foliage
Viburnum plicatum 'Popcorn'

Supporting ingredient
Tatarian honeysuckle (*Lonicera tatarica*)

Textural ingredient
Helleborus orientalis

Supporting flowers
Daffodil 'Breezand Tristar'
Daffodil 'Snowboard'

Focal flower
Tulip 'Green Star'

Airy accents
Daffodil 'Sailboat'
Wild heuchera

120

Daffodil 'Breezand Tristar'

Tulip 'Green Star'

Tatarian honeysuckle
(*Lonicera tatarica*)

Daffodil 'Sailboat'

Daffodil
'Snowboard'

Helleborus orientalis

Viburnum plicatum
'Popcorn'

Wild heuchera

Sherbet-Toned Centerpiece

Behind our funky old house sits a one-car garage that I've transformed into a bright, cheerful flower studio. It has uneven floors; thin, rattling windows; and so many cracks in the walls that plants often make their way inside to bloom. When I first took over this space, I was embarrassed by how rundown it looked on the outside, so I planted a dozen heirloom climbing roses and vines all around the perimeter in hopes that it would eventually be swallowed up in a sea of blooms. The plants flourished, and now I'm continually cutting away branches from the windows so I can still see outside.

Right outside the studio's back door is the most glorious honeysuckle vine that my eighty-five-year-old neighbor, Louise, gifted me shortly after we moved in. At the tail end of every spring, it explodes into a cloud of fragrant flowers, filling the studio and our backyard with the sweetest scent. I'm always shocked by how vigorous this vine remains, even though we cut from it for nearly every late-spring bouquet.

Inspired by this treasured honeysuckle, I wanted flowers to complement its two-toned blossoms, so I combined it with the last of the blush pink and buttercream yellow ranunculus from our greenhouse. Filipendula buds, the veining of the hellebores, and new growth of blueberry and snowberry foliage help carry pink throughout the arrangement. To bring in a tad more yellow and a bit of sparkle, I threaded in airy heuchera flowers, and I used a vintage footed bowl from our local antique store to ground this ethereal, feminine arrangement.

INGREDIENTS

Structural foliage
Snowberry 'Hancock'

Supporting ingredient
Blueberry 'Duke' foliage

Textural ingredient
Honeysuckle 'Munster'

Supporting flower
Helleborus orientalis

Focal flower
Ranunculus Pastel Mix

Airy accents
Heuchera 'Amber Waves'
Filipendula ulmaria

126

Snowberry 'Hancock'

Heuchera 'Amber Waves'

Helleborus orientalis

Blueberry 'Duke' foliage

Filipendula ulmaria

Ranunculus Pastel Mix

Honeysuckle 'Munster'

Hints of Blush Vignette

Narcissus are the very first flowers to bloom on our farm in spring, and after a long rainy winter, they're a sight for sore eyes. These gems have gotten a bad rap because many people associate them with the glaring school-bus yellow, dollar-a-dozen bunches from grocery stores. But they're actually amazingly diverse: besides varying shades of yellow, some have peach, salmon, white, and apricot blooms. Each stem might have a huge trumpet-shaped flower or many miniature ones. Some are fragrant; others could easily be mistaken for peonies or orchids. In addition to being one of the first spring blooms, these beauties are also extremely easy to grow, they multiply, they're deer proof, and they take harsh weather in stride. Over time, they've earned their place as one of my all-time favorite groups of flowers.

We've been growing daffodils—a type of narcissus—for more than a decade, and we're always on the lookout for new treasures to add to our collection. Recently we trialed more than sixty varieties, searching for ones with unique colors and scents that are also good for cutting. I thought we might find a dozen we'd want to add, but we discovered more than forty new favorites—and I'm already making plans for our next trial patch.

Because daffodils bloom so early, there aren't many opportunities to mix them with other flowers or foliage when they're at their peak, so I love to display them on their own or in groupings to highlight their unique characteristics. Over the years, I've gathered a collection of vintage bottles and jars that I keep specifically for showing off daffodils.

INGREDIENTS (ALL FOCAL FLOWERS)

Daffodil 'Apricot Whirl'

Daffodil 'Precocious'

Daffodil 'Accent'

Daffodil 'Coral Light'

Daffodil 'Sunny Girlfriend'

Daffodil 'Extravaganza'

Daffodil 'Prosecco'

Daffodil 'High Society'

Daffodil 'Delnashaugh'

Daffodil 'Passionale'

Daffodil 'Katie Heath'

Daffodil 'Pink Wonder'

Daffodil 'Bell Song'

Daffodil 'Erlicheer'

Daffodil 'Snowboard'

Daffodil 'Apricot Whirl'

Daffodil 'Coral Light'

Daffodil 'Accent'

Daffodil 'Extravaganza'

Daffodil 'Precocious'

Daffodil 'Sunny Girlfriend'

Daffodil 'Delnashaugh'

Daffodil 'Bell Song'

Daffodil 'Passionale'

Daffodil 'Snowboard'

Daffodil 'High Society'

Daffodil 'Pink Wonder'

Daffodil 'Katie Heath'

Daffodil 'Prosecco'

Daffodil 'Erlicheer'

Periwinkle and Buttercream Posy

In spring, more than any other season, I find myself noticing the tiniest details in nature, and pansies, a type of viola, are one of my favorite miniature blooms this time of year. They're among the first plants nurseries offer for sale in the season, and it's no wonder they're so popular. They're cold hardy, thrive with minimal care, can be grown in containers, and self-sow freely around the garden year after year. But more than anything, their cheerful, smiling faces are irresistible.

In recent years, plant breeders have devoted a lot of energy to developing pansies with new and exciting traits. You can now find numerous varieties boasting ruffled petals, muted antique colors, and a trailing growth habit that produces longer stems ideal for flower arranging. Recently, we conducted our first ever pansy trial on the farm, growing more than forty varieties with distinctive characteristics in search of the very best to add to our shop's seed offerings. I knew there were a lot of amazing choices, but I underestimated just how many of these treasures I would fall in love with. Narrowing the list of favorites has been nearly impossible!

Early in the season, when the stems are still very short, I love to display pansies in tiny bottles along my kitchen windowsill to admire their unique traits up close. Then, as the days grow longer and their stems start to stretch, it's fun to tuck them into as many arrangements as possible. I think one of the sweetest color combinations early in the season is periwinkle blue and buttercream yellow. In this bouquet, the unripe blueberries, geraniums, and forget-me-nots all carry a lovely gray-blue undertone, and bicolor blue-and-yellow pansies bridge these to buttercream Iceland poppies, honeysuckle buds, and roses. This cheerful, sweetly scented pastel bouquet is brimming with so many of my favorite delicate spring flowers.

INGREDIENTS

Structural foliage
Blueberry 'Duke'

Supporting ingredient
Garden mignonette

Textural ingredient
Honeysuckle 'Scentsation'

Supporting flowers
Pansy 'Majestic Giants II Marina Shades'
Viola 'Gem Heavenly Blue'
Pansy 'Cool Wave Lemon Improved'
Pansy 'Cool Wave Blueberry Swirl'
Rose 'Ghislaine de Féligonde'
Pansy 'Frizzle Sizzle Lemonade'
Pansy 'Frizzle Sizzle Yellow-Blue Swirl'
Pansy 'ColorMax Icy Blue'
Sweet pea 'Oban Bay'
Geranium 'Mrs. Kendall Clark'

Focal flower
Iceland poppy Meadow Pastels

Airy accent
Forget-me-nots

138

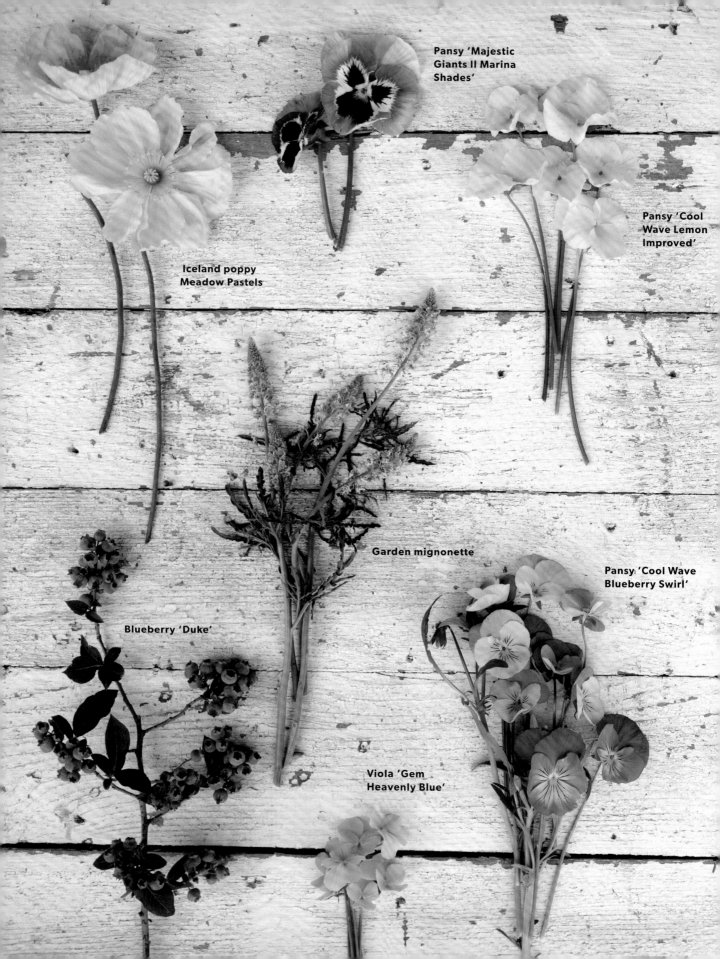

Pansy 'Majestic Giants II Marina Shades'

Pansy 'Cool Wave Lemon Improved'

Iceland poppy Meadow Pastels

Garden mignonette

Pansy 'Cool Wave Blueberry Swirl'

Blueberry 'Duke'

Viola 'Gem Heavenly Blue'

Honeysuckle 'Scentsation'

Sweet pea 'Oban Bay'

Pansy 'Frizzle Sizzle Yellow-Blue Swirl'

Pansy 'Frizzle Sizzle Lemonade'

Forget-me-nots

Pansy 'ColorMax Icy Blue'

Rose 'Ghislaine de Féligonde'

Geranium 'Mrs. Kendall Clark'

Wild and Refined Bridal Bouquet

When I was just out of high school, I worked for the most inspiring artist and garden designer, Jana Belisle, who transformed tiny urban plots in Seattle into beautiful wild sanctuaries that didn't feel like they belonged in the middle of a bustling city. She taught me about the two things I value most: motherhood and gardening. Jana wasn't afraid of wildness, and unlike any other gardener I'd previously known, she welcomed a bit of chaos instead of always trying to control nature.

I worked with Jana for a couple of years before transplanting to the Skagit Valley. As a going-away present, she gave me a potted 'Cecile Brunner' rose to tuck into my new garden. I planted it right next to the front door, hoping it would amble up the side of the house and spill over our archway like I'd seen in so many romantic photos. 'Cecile Brunner' has since swallowed up the front of the house and is even sneaking toward the top of the chimney. As spring fades to summer, the sprawling plant is covered in a sea of fluffy, cherry blossom–like flowers exuding a peppery, old rose scent. While the plant is massive, the blooms are petite and feminine, and I find the best way to enjoy them is up close.

One of the biggest lessons I learned from Jana was how to marry the wild and the refined. This traditional bridal bouquet is filled with expected wedding flowers like lilacs, roses, ranunculus, and anemones. But to keep it from looking too predictable, I mixed in common garden weeds as a nod to what's happening in the field at this time of year—a closer look reveals white clover, grasses, rye, and wild sorrel along with blueberry foliage and flowering ninebark. By combining ingredients from opposite ends of the spectrum, I've found that you almost always get beautiful and unexpected results.

INGREDIENTS

Structural foliage
Blueberry 'Duke'

Supporting ingredients
Lilac 'Primrose'
Ninebark 'Diablo'
Spirea 'Snowmound'
Rockrose buds

Textural ingredients
Wild sorrel (*Rumex acetosella*)
Rye

Supporting flowers
Lupine 'The Pages'
Rose 'Cecile Brunner'

Focal flowers
Ranunculus 'Pink Picotee'
Anemone 'Galilee Black and White'

Airy accents
White clover
White campion (*Silene latifolia*)
Filipendula ulmaria
Grass gone to seed

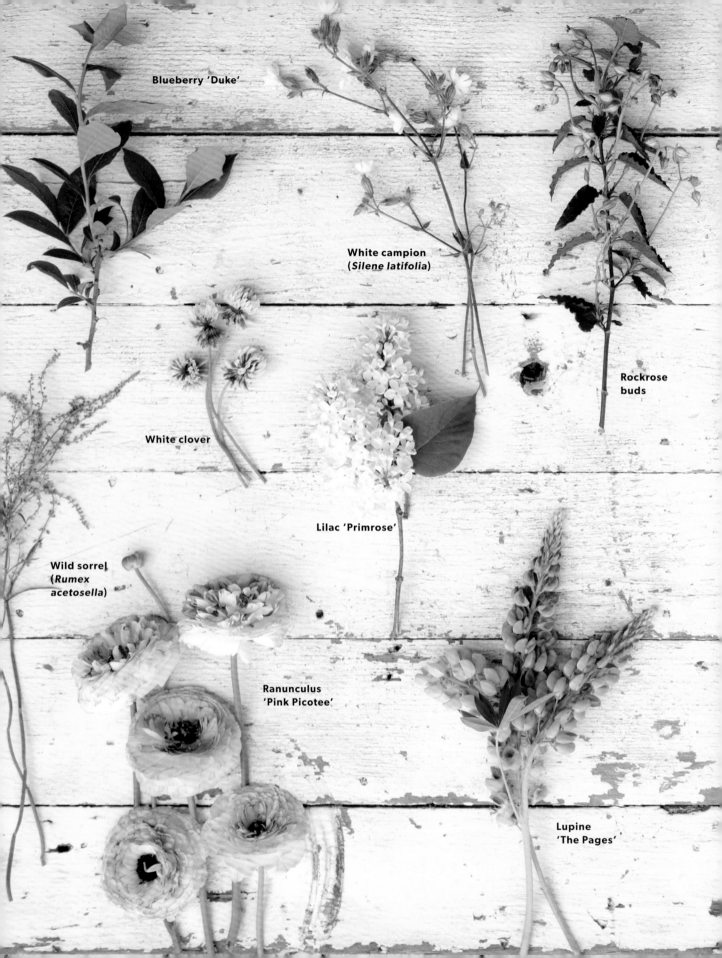

Blueberry 'Duke'

White campion
(*Silene latifolia*)

Rockrose
buds

White clover

Lilac 'Primrose'

Wild sorrel
(*Rumex
acetosella*)

Ranunculus
'Pink Picotee'

Lupine
'The Pages'

Ninebark
'Diablo'

*Filipendula
ulmaria*

Grass
gone to seed

Anemone
'Galilee Black
and White'

Rose
'Cecile Brunner'

Spirea
'Snowmound'

Rye

Clouds of Purple En Masse

So many people I've met have stories about lilacs; there are few other flowers that elicit such a strong emotional response. Give someone a handful of fresh lilacs and they immediately start rattling off memories, often tied to a grandmother, an aunt, or a childhood experience. When not flowering, the shrubs themselves are very unassuming and easy to overlook, but for the two weeks that they bloom in spring, they're a glorious sight to behold.

Years ago, when my kids were small and we'd just moved to the country, I had the good fortune of meeting Carl and Waverly Jaegel. Waverly is a rosarian by trade, and these two passionate gardeners have turned their ten-acre homestead into a mini paradise filled with fruit trees, chickens, hundreds of rose varieties, and dozens of rare heirloom lilacs.

Every spring I find a way to get invited over to harvest from their lilac grove, often trading seeds or dahlia tubers for the flowers. On my annual harvest day, I try to arrive just after sunrise so I can fill the back of the car while the weather is still cool. Even after all these years of Waverly reassuring me I can take as much as I want, I still feel a little guilty picking so many. They're so beautiful, fragrant, and fleeting that I find myself holding my breath when I'm harvesting. It's one of the best days of the season.

To me, there's nothing more beautiful than a big ol' vase overflowing with billowy lilacs, and I rarely mix them with other ingredients, since I've always found that they look best on their own. With so many gorgeous varieties to work with here, I didn't want to limit myself to one particular color, so I combined all of the lavender, pink, blue, and purple varieties that I harvested at Waverly's. The branches are top heavy and can easily topple a vase, so I chose a heavy Farmhouse Pottery beehive crock to arrange in.

INGREDIENTS (ALL FOCAL FLOWERS)

Lilac 'Krasavitsa Moskvy'

Lilac 'Katherine Havemeyer'

Lilac 'Michel Buchner'

Lilac 'Champlain'

Lilac 'Blue Delight'

Lilac 'Bluets'

Lilac 'Yankee Doodle'

Lilac 'Blue Danube'

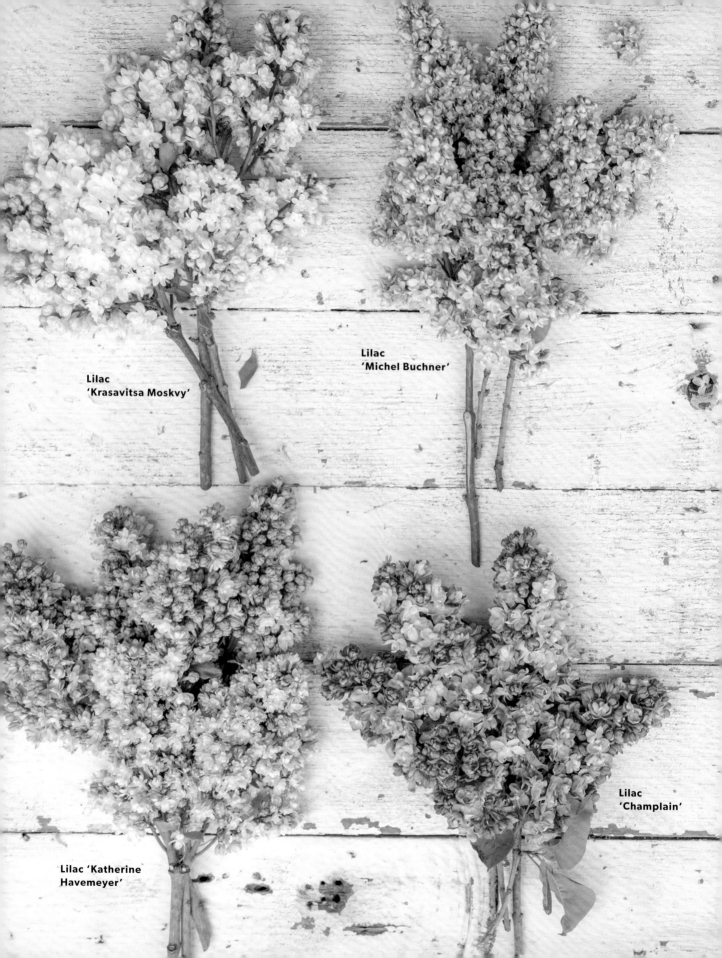

Lilac 'Krasavitsa Moskvy'

Lilac 'Michel Buchner'

Lilac 'Champlain'

Lilac 'Katherine Havemeyer'

Lilac 'Blue Delight'

Lilac 'Yankee Doodle'

Lilac 'Bluets'

Lilac 'Blue Danube'

Flower Crown

Flower crowns are the perfect accessories for any special occasion, and assembling them is a fun activity for parties or showers. With a few simple floral supplies and a basic understanding of the technique, flower crowns are quite easy to make.

To create the most beautiful crown, gather a mix of sturdy flowers and foliage, such as spray roses and plants with leathery leaves, plus textural accents such as pods and tiny berries. If you want your finished crown to be delicate and airy, choose petite ingredients; if you prefer a fuller look, choose larger, chunkier material. When choosing flowers and foliage, look for ones that will hold up well out of water—when in doubt, test the ingredients by leaving a few samples on the counter out of water, and see what still looks good after a few hours.

If you are making multiple crowns, place piles of flowers and foliage on a cookie sheet so that you can approach the task like an assembly line, grabbing one stem from each pile quickly. When wiring ingredients, use a thin gauge wire (my favorite is 22-gauge) because it crimps easily and doesn't add extra bulk to the finished crown. Floral tape becomes sticky only when stretched, so be sure to pull with gentle pressure when wrapping stems and wire. Also, wrap the tape at a slight angle as you go to minimize bulk and for the best adhesion.

If you're not going to be wearing your crown right away, you can store it for 24 to 36 hours wrapped in plastic in the produce section of your refrigerator.

TO MAKE A FLOWER CROWN, YOU WILL NEED:

Supplies

2 ft (60 cm) paper-covered wire

Mix of sturdy flowers and foliage, plus textural accents—you'll need 48 to 90 stems of ingredients to make a crown, and it's always good to have some extra in case anything breaks

Ten 6 in (15 cm) pieces 22-gauge floral wire for anything that needs individual wiring

Roll of floral tape, light green preferred

6 to 8 ft (1.8 to 2.4 m) decorative ribbon (optional)

157

Ingredients

Ranunculus 'La Belle Pastel Lemon'

Mock orange buds (*Philadelphus*)

Helleborus 'Pirouette'

Rose 'Malvern Hills'

Rose 'Darlow's Enigma'

Heuchera 'Amber Waves'

Blueberry 'Duke'

Raspberry 'Tulameen'

Privet flowers

Columbine seedpods

Apple foliage

1. To determine the crown's circumference, wrap the paper-covered wire around your head where you want it to rest. Allow for an extra 2 in (5 cm) on either side for fastening together later. Make a loop on one end and keep the other end straight. Straighten out the paper-covered wire before adding the ingredients.

2. Cut all of the ingredients into "bite-size" pieces, making sure to leave 2 in (5 cm) of the stem remaining. Organize the ingredients in piles.

3. Individually wire any heavy or wilt-prone flowers, such as dahlias and ranunculus. Crimp a straight piece of wire to form a hairpin. Carefully slip it through the center of the flower head and tape the wire ends and stem together.

4. Individually wire thick-stemmed leaves. This will reduce the bulk and make the flower crown lighter. Make a hairpin with floral wire and slip it through the leaf on each side of the vein. Tape the wire ends and stem together.

5. Assemble 12 to 15 bundles of roughly 4 to 6 stems each, using a mixture of ingredients with flowers, foliage, and textural elements. Wrap the top 1 in (2.5 cm) of each bundle's stems together with floral tape, gently stretching the tape as you work so it becomes sticky and adheres to itself.

6. To create the crown, take a bundle and lay it along the paper-covered wire at the looped end. Wrap floral tape around the bundle and the wire a few times until secure.

7. Add the remaining bundles, facing them in the same direction as the first and placing them so that each hides the previous bundle's stem ends, until the paper-covered wire is obscured.

8. Place the crown on your head and secure the ends by feeding the straight end of the wire through the loop and twisting to secure it. If you like, tie lengths of ribbon to the back.

Summer

Summer is the busiest time of year on the farm. While our part of Washington state is generally cool and damp, this season generally brings two glorious months of warm, dry weather. These conditions, combined with our northern location and long days, produce an ideal environment for growing huge, beautiful plants. While spring is filled with so much hope and possibility, summer is incredibly rewarding because that's when all of our hard work starts really bearing fruit. As far as the eye can see, our fields are a sea of color, shapes, and textures.

This time of year, I get up really early and head out to the field as soon as it's light enough to see. At the start of the season, the garden roses and peonies are in their prime, heaving their heavy blooms into the paths, creating the most abundant display. From there, it's a rapid succession of variety after variety putting on a show. The farm is literally humming with activity, not just with our busy farm crew, but also with birds and pollinators. Hummingbirds start their work at dawn and spend the day zooming around the fields drinking nectar. I've noticed that their favorite crop is flowering tobacco, so we grow seven different varieties just for them. And now that our plants have grown enough to resist scratching and pecking, we let our bantam chickens venture out into the garden. Few sights are more adorable than our fluffy flock hunting for insects up and down the rows.

In the greenhouses, our tomato plants are covered with fruit, which we both snack on throughout the day and pick for flower arrangements. Our family harvests almost daily from our vegetable patch, and I love to pluck handfuls of edibles, like beans, peas, and tomatillos, to combine with flowers.

There is so much beauty pouring out of the garden on any given day that the abundance can feel overwhelming. It's nearly impossible to stay on top of the harvesting, let alone capture the beauty on camera. Each year we trial between two hundred and three hundred new varieties, looking for additional treasures to add to our lineup. I have strict criteria for evaluating each variety, including good stem length, disease resistance, beautiful coloring, and, if possible, a pleasant fragrance. I spend a full day every week walking the farm, taking notes, and evaluating each variety in the trial area. It's my favorite summer task, hands down.

As summer comes to an end and the days gradually grow shorter, the once-green fields start to dry out and fade. Any unpicked blossoms begin to set seed, signaling that autumn is just around the corner.

Coral Infusion Statement Piece

I can't quite recall how I first met Geraldine Kildow, but it feels like we've known each other forever. She is one of the most joyful and passionate flower farmers I know, and every time I talk to her, my love of flowers grows even stronger. Two decades ago, while working as a full-time nurse practitioner, Geraldine started planning ahead for her retirement and carved out a space on her property to devote to one main crop: her favorite flowers, peonies.

At the end of every June, we make the annual pilgrimage to spend an evening with Geraldine among her flowers. Her love of life and the blooms that she grows is contagious. It seems like the only thing she loves more than the peonies is watching people experience their magic firsthand. Even though I live on a flower farm and get to enjoy blooms all the time, picking Geraldine's peonies is the best harvesting day of the entire year. There are so many beautiful choices spilling out of her fields that choosing a favorite is nearly impossible, but I always find myself coming back to the raspberry- and coral-toned varieties: 'Coral Charm', 'Pink Hawaiian Coral', and 'Cytherea'.

Peonies bloom just as the wild roses are flowering and the early perennials are putting on a show. For this arrangement, I paired my treasured Frances Palmer footed vase with ingredients in soft, feminine colors. The sweet peas' blush edges pick up the tones of the peonies and garden roses, while autumn ferns' copper-touched fronds accent the ninebark seedpods. Smokebush lends an antique quality to the whole display.

INGREDIENTS

Structural foliage
Ninebark with seedpods
(*Physocarpus opufolius*)

Supporting ingredient
Smokebush 'Grace'

Textural ingredient
Autumn fern

Supporting flowers
Spray rose
Rose 'Abraham Darby'
Rose 'Penelope'
Rose 'Sally Holmes'

Focal flower
Peony 'Coral Charm'

Airy accent
Sweet pea 'Mollie Rilstone'

164

Spray rose

Rose 'Abraham Darby'

Autumn fern

Sweet pea 'Mollie Rilstone'

Rose 'Penelope'

Rose 'Sally Holmes'

Smokebush
'Grace'

Peony 'Coral Charm'

Ninebark
with seedpods
(*Physocarpus
opufolius*)

Meadow-Inspired Centerpiece

In high summer, our fields are literally a sea of flowers, and when I walk the rows, I have to part the waves of waist-high plants to wade through them. In early August, the perennial section is in its prime, and echinacea stands out as one of the stars. Of all the perennial flowers that we grow, it is one of the most loved by the beneficial creatures living on the farm, from the hummingbirds to the honeybees. All day long the rows of echinacea are literally buzzing with pollinators. At the end of a long day, I love to sit in the perennial patch where, if I keep still long enough, I notice that everything is moving, humming, and vibrating. The stress of the day dissipates and I become more in tune with nature, which always helps put things in perspective.

One of my favorite challenges is to elevate even the most common flowers—those that are often overlooked, such as cosmos and daisies—by combining them with more refined, romantic ingredients like garden roses. The tension formed between these opposites always tends to kick-start conversations as people stop to comment on the elements they recognize. White echinacea, a common native flower, inspired this bouquet that embraces the blooms of peak summer. From there, I hunted around the farm and gathered all of the more refined white flowers I could find, including PeeGee hydrangeas, clematis, and mignonette. To offset these, I chose a few textural ingredients that aren't commonly thought of for bouquets, including immature raspberries and pokeweed seedpods. To retain a loose, airy quality, I gave each of the flowers room to breathe and express their individual nature.

For my vessel, I chose a beautiful vintage mixing bowl from my favorite antique store. It's so well worn that the glaze is partially rubbed off, exposing a linen-colored base that echoes the echinacea centers and the soft gold of the unripe raspberries.

INGREDIENTS

Structural foliage
Rosa multiflora foliage

Supporting ingredients
Pokeweed
Hydrangea 'Bobo'
Hydrangea 'Little Lamb'
Raspberry 'Tulameen'

Textural ingredient
Clematis 'Paul Farges' (Summer Snow)

Supporting flower
Echinacea 'Coconut Lime'

Focal flower
Echinacea 'White Swan'

Airy accent
White mignonette

Pokeweed

Hydrangea
'Bobo'

Echinacea
'Coconut
Lime'

Hydrangea
'Little Lamb'

Echinacea
'White
Swan'

Rosa
multiflora
foliage

White
mignonette

Raspberry
'Tulameen'

Clematis
'Paul Farges'
(Summer
Snow)

Moody Blues Vignette

I'm constantly asked what my favorite flower is, and choosing is nearly impossible. But if I could pick only one, it would definitely be sweet peas. In addition to being extremely fragrant and coming in a huge array of colors, these blooms evoke intense nostalgia; I often hear people recounting favorite memories related to them. Sweet peas were the gateway flower that got me into this adventure—the first blooms I grew and sold, which led to starting a farm, which eventually grew to include floral design and teaching.

The first year I grew sweet peas in our garden, I planted two varieties, one on either side of a walkway down the center of the veggie patch. The following year I grew twelve varieties, and the year after that, I upped my game and conducted an official trial that included more than twenty-five long-stemmed English varieties that are most suited for cutting. Sweet peas have been a mainstay crop at our farm since the beginning, and over the years we've grown well over a hundred different varieties. Getting seeds for these demure blooms has become rather difficult, as drought in the areas where they are commercially produced has caused a worldwide seed shortage. Over the past couple of years, we've been learning how to grow sweet peas not only for cut flowers but also for seed, in hopes that someday we'll be able to make these beauties easily accessible to gardeners everywhere.

Sweet peas come in a dazzling rainbow of hues, including red, coral, magenta, pink, white, ivory, purple, lavender, blue, almost black, and numerous streaked and flaked options. I'm consistently drawn to the cool blue and purple tones, and in this vignette I highlight all of my favorites in those shades, along with a hint of white for good measure. While sweet peas are a wonderful addition to mixed bouquets, more often than not I display them on their own for the most impact and also the most fragrance.

INGREDIENTS (ALL FOCAL FLOWERS)

Sweet pea 'Blue Shift'

Sweet pea 'Our Harry'

Sweet pea 'Lady Nicholson'

Sweet pea 'Nimbus'

Sweet pea 'Oban Bay'

Sweet pea 'Erewhon'

Sweet pea 'Ethel Grace'

Sweet pea 'Triple G'

Sweet pea 'Enchante'

Sweet pea 'Charlie's Angel'

Sweet pea 'Wild Swan'

Sweet pea 'North Shore'

176

Sweet pea 'Blue Shift'

Sweet pea 'Nimbus'

Sweet pea 'Lady Nicholson'

Sweet pea 'Erewhon'

Sweet pea 'Our Harry'

Sweet pea 'Oban Bay'

Sweet pea
'Charlie's
Angel'

Sweet pea
'Ethel Grace'

Sweet pea
'North Shore'

Sweet pea
'Enchante'

Sweet pea
'Triple G'

Sweet pea
'Wild Swan'

Farm-to-Table Posy

The first year I grew a vegetable garden after we moved from the city to the country, I was so excited about having room to spread out that I got carried away. I spent the winter combing every seed catalog I could get my hands on and ordered fifty varieties of tomato seeds. Not having a dedicated seed-starting space, I planted indoors and pushed our dining table against the wall so the warmth from the baseboard heaters would help germinate the seeds. What I didn't take into account was that, when our house was warm, the organic fish-based fertilizer I'd mixed in the potting soil would make our home smell like a fish market on a hot day. Fortunately, my husband, Chris, was a good sport, and because it was too cold to move my plants outside, we just lived with it. Once the weather warmed, we tilled up a huge section of the lawn and devoted it all to tomatoes.

I had high hopes of turning my harvest into homemade salsa, ketchup, and tomato sauce, but nature had other things in mind. While I had a lot of experience growing things in the landscape, I was very new to vegetable gardening and didn't know that each type of plant had special needs. Here in Washington state, where the weather is very damp, tomatoes grown outdoors without any type of protection are very susceptible to blight. All summer I staked, pruned, and fed my patch, which quickly became a fruit-laden jungle—but shortly after the plants started bearing fruit, I woke up one morning to find that the foliage on many of my tomatoes had turned black, and within a matter of days the whole patch was hit by blight. My canning and homesteading dreams were dashed, and this was one of my first big tastes of what was in store for me as a gardener. You try your best, but ultimately Mother Nature

is in charge. The following spring, Chris built me a little greenhouse for seed starting and tomato growing, and since then we've successfully grown healthy plants every season.

I love incorporating edibles into arrangements, and tomatoes are my top pick. A cluster of cherry tomatoes tumbling out of a vase is guaranteed to stop people in their tracks every time. This bouquet is filled with ingredients from our veggie patch that you would normally see on your dinner plate, making for a fun, whimsical display that embodies the abundance of midsummer.

INGREDIENTS

Structural foliage
Scented geranium 'Attar of Rose'

Supporting ingredients
Greek oregano
Nasturtium 'Gleam Salmon'
Nasturtium 'Cherry Rose Jewel'
Yarrow 'Terracotta'
Pennycress

Textural ingredients
Tomato 'Candyland Red'
Tomato 'Red Currant'
Tomato 'Cherry Roma'

Supporting flower
Zinnia 'Profusion Deep Apricot'

Focal flower
Zinnia 'Mazurkia'

Airy accent
Cape fuchsia 'Salmon Leap'

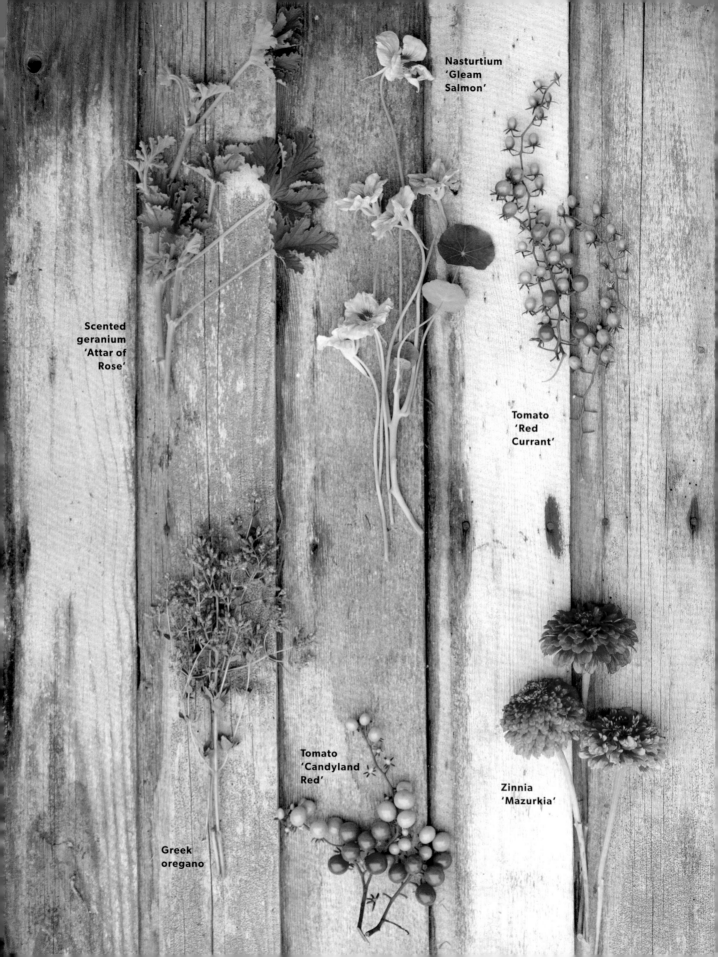

Nasturtium
'Gleam
Salmon'

Scented
geranium
'Attar of
Rose'

Tomato
'Red
Currant'

Tomato
'Candyland
Red'

Zinnia
'Mazurkia'

Greek
oregano

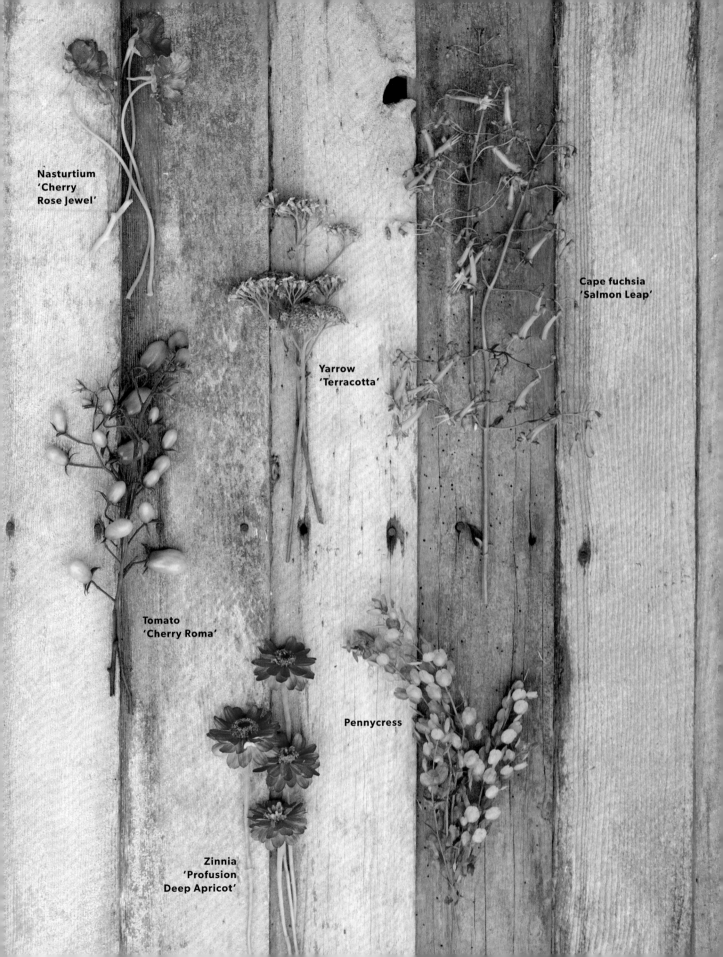

Nasturtium
'Cherry
Rose Jewel'

Cape fuchsia
'Salmon Leap'

Yarrow
'Terracotta'

Tomato
'Cherry Roma'

Pennycress

Zinnia
'Profusion
Deep Apricot'

Summer Bounty Hand-Tied Market Bouquet

Making and selling hand-tied bouquets was one of the early stepping-stones that helped us grow our little backyard cutting garden into a full-fledged flower farm. Once I got the hang of raising flowers, I had more than I could use for the weddings and events I designed, so I started looking for other ways to share our farm's bounty. That's when we learned that the Whole Foods chain in Seattle—which at the time was an up-and-coming high-end grocery store in our area—was looking for local farmers whose products they might offer. The week their request went out, at least a dozen people forwarded it to me. The thought of selling our flowers to such a huge corporate chain was extremely intimidating, but this seemed like an opportunity I couldn't pass up.

I met with the regional buyer, and it became clear that making market bouquets would allow us to sell an insane amount of flowers from our farm. For eight years, each week from mid-May through early October, my family and I cranked out between three hundred and four hundred of these bouquets. At this point, I've made more than forty thousand of them and have refined the process so it takes me less than one minute to assemble, bunch, and wrap without even thinking.

For me, the best part of putting together a market bouquet is choosing its ingredients. This one highlights two of my favorite butterscotch-colored dahlias, along with some beautiful golden celosia. I incorporated bright green bells of Ireland, limelight hydrangeas, cress, and parsley seedpods to offset the warm sherbet-toned blooms. To add an unexpected pop, I wove in a few airy sprays of periwinkle delphinium. You can never go wrong with this clean, fresh color palette.

INGREDIENTS

Structural foliage
Bells of Ireland

Supporting ingredients
Yarrow 'Summer Berries'
Hydrangea 'Limelight'

Textural ingredients
Celosia Pampas Plume Mix
Celosia Supercrest Mix
Cress 'Wrinkled Crinkled'
Parsley seed heads

Supporting flowers
Delphinium 'Fashion Lavender'
Elephant garlic (*Allium*) blossom

Focal flowers
Dahlia 'Lakeview Peach Fuzz'
Dahlia 'Valley Tawny'

Airy accents
Pink foxtail barley
Ornamental grass 'Frosted Explosion'

Bells of
Ireland

Celosia
Pampas
Plume Mix

Dahlia
'Lakeview
Peach Fuzz'

Delphinium
'Fashion
Lavender'

Pink
foxtail
barley

Celosia
Supercrest
Mix

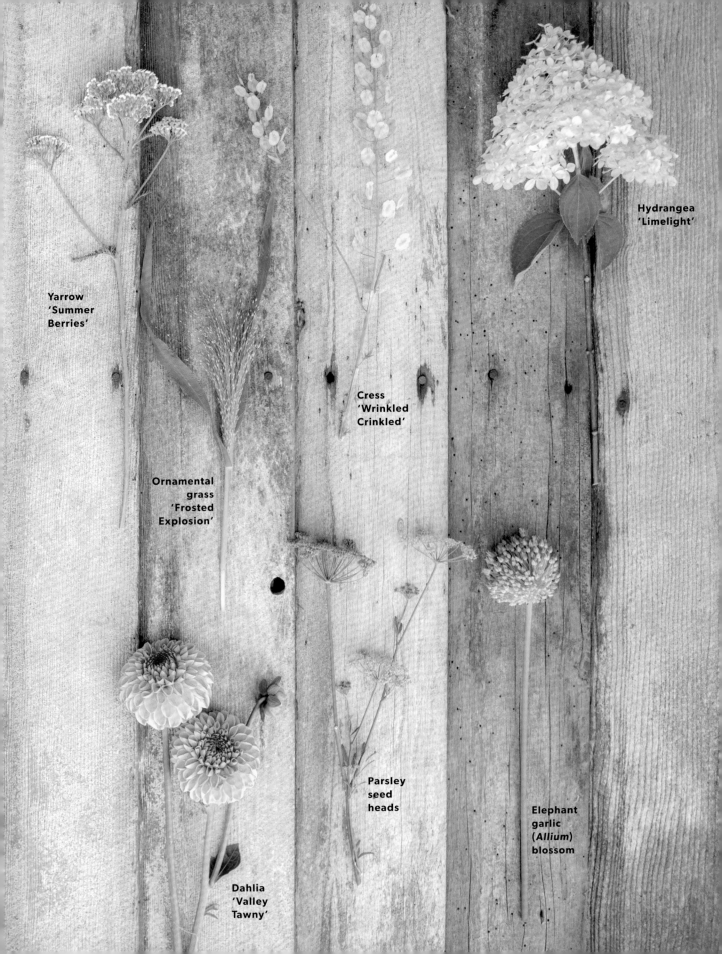

Yarrow
'Summer
Berries'

Cress
'Wrinkled
Crinkled'

Hydrangea
'Limelight'

Ornamental
grass
'Frosted
Explosion'

Parsley
seed
heads

Elephant
garlic
(*Allium*)
blossom

Dahlia
'Valley
Tawny'

Fields of Pink En Masse

Each year, we get hundreds of emails from beginning gardeners asking which cut flowers are easiest to grow from seed. Without fail, our answer is always cosmos. Besides their being extremely easy to grow from seed, I love how abundantly cosmos flower. The more you pick from them, the more they bloom, so it's important to harvest from your plants every couple of days, never letting the flowers go to seed, which would signal the plant to shut down for the season.

There's a type of cosmos for everyone, from knee-high varieties bred to provide color at the front of a border to towering giants, intended for cut flowers, that grow as tall as 7 ft (2.1 m) in our field. Blooms come in a dazzling array of colors, including cranberry, rose, blush, pure white, apricot, and iridescent mauve, and there are also a handful of intriguing varieties with streaked petals that look more like candy than flowers. Some cosmos also have unusual bloom shapes and sizes. While standard varieties look similar to daisies, with a single ring of petals radiating out from their golden centers, some—like the ones I used in this arrangement—have fluffy, ruffled petals, and still others have fluted, tubular petals. Beneficial insects love all of them, and picking cosmos before the bees pollinate them can sometimes feel like a full-time job.

Cosmos last a long time in bouquets, provided you harvest just as their petals are unfurling and before the bees have pollinated them. Every year, we grow hundreds to use in our mixed bouquets but one of my favorite ways to display this hardworking flower is en masse. Here I've combined all of the colors in the Double Click series, in a Farmhouse Pottery confit jar, for a cheerful, lovely display. If you haven't grown cosmos before, I hope this inspires you to give them a try.

INGREDIENTS (ALL FOCAL FLOWERS)

Cosmos 'Double Click Snow Puff'

Cosmos 'Double Click Cranberries'

Cosmos 'Double Click Bicolor Violet'

Cosmos 'Double Click Bicolor Rose Bonbon'

Cosmos 'Double Click Bicolor Pink'

194

Cosmos 'Double Click Bicolor Pink'

Cosmos 'Double Click Bicolor Violet'

Cosmos 'Double Click Cranberries'

Cosmos 'Double Click Bicolor Rose Bonbon'

Cosmos 'Double Click Snow Puff'

Wrist Corsage

For the longest time, just the mention of wrist corsages would make me shudder. I created flowers for hundreds of weddings, and I would always save the wrist corsages for the very last because they were time consuming and tricky to execute. Plus, no matter how hard I tried or what flowers I used, they always looked dated. This all changed the day I met Susan McLeary, affectionately referred to as Passionflower Sue. Sue has made it her personal mission to revolutionize wearable flowers and elevate the lowly wrist corsage. Sue taught me the technique shown here, and I no longer dread making corsages—I actually look forward to this fun and creative pursuit.

For the most beautiful and long-lasting corsage, it's important to select a mix of sturdy ingredients that will hold well without water. Flowers that can be dried, like strawflower and globe amaranth (gomphrena), and textural elements like pods and rose hips, are great candidates. Floral adhesive gets messy, so be sure to cover your workspace appropriately. It's also important to have a container for the glue to stand upright and a paper plate or piece of scrap cardboard for dipping ingredients into the glue.

These corsages can be made a day or two in advance, but they must be kept cool in the produce section of a refrigerator in a sealed container. Once you try making them, you'll be hooked and will soon start making up occasions just so you can wear one of these beautiful creations.

TO MAKE A WRIST CORSAGE, YOU WILL NEED:

Supplies

Mix of sturdy flowers and foliage, plus textural and airy accents

1½ in (4 cm) wide brass cuff

Oasis floral adhesive

Dried moss

Paper plate or scrap paper for glue dipping

Flower ingredients

Strawflower Apricot Mix

'Salmon Queen' pincushion flower buds

Hydrangea 'Quick Fire' blossoms

Textural ingredients

Unripe raspberries

Celosia

Crabapples

Rose hips

Pokeweed

Mignonette pods

Celosia Supercrest Mix

199

1. Prepare the ingredients by removing the stems from all flowers, and cutting the textural ingredients down into small pieces.

2. Holding the cuff with one hand, swirl a small amount of glue in the center of the cuff, leaving 1 ½ in (4 cm) on either end bare and the outer edges clear.

3. Stick a thin layer of dried moss over the glue and press down to adhere. This will create the base for all of the other flowers.

4. Apply a generous amount of glue to the back of the flowers.

5. Before applying the flowers, dab a little more glue onto the moss where you will place the flowers. Press the flowers firmly to the cuff and apply pressure with your thumb and forefinger. Allow to dry for at least 30 seconds. Continue until the flowers are placed and secure.

6. Dip the backs of textural ingredients in a puddle of glue, set in place on the cuff, and hold them for about 30 seconds until dry.

7. Continue to glue on textural ingredients around the flowers, filling in any large gaps.

8. Finish the corsage by gluing on any remaining textural ingredients.

Autumn

I'm always caught off guard by how quickly everything changes in autumn. While our climate is considered mild compared to many others, this season comes on so fast, it's as if someone somewhere flipped a switch: one minute we're enjoying the late summer garden, and the next we're bundled up in rain gear and boots. Almost overnight, the shadows grow longer, and the light takes on a more golden quality.

Once I see cranberry freckles appear on hydrangea flowers and notice the burgundy cast on viburnum leaves, I know that summer has officially come to an end. As the rain returns, the seasonal transition picks up speed. Early mornings are dewy and cold, and spiders spin webs across every doorway and path, so I often carry a stick to gently clear the way. The songbirds seem to be especially active, scavenging for all of the ripening seeds, nuts, and fruit.

By late October, frost has arrived and all of the annuals in our field have turned black. By then, the trees are smothered in gold and the hedgerows are ablaze with brilliant color. The first heavy storm strips the trees, leaving behind drifts of glowing foliage that we collect as mulch for the garden.

No matter how many years I've been growing, I never get used to how rapidly the landscape shifts this time of year. My once overflowing flowerbeds melt into a rotted, soggy mess in a matter of weeks. It's a bittersweet time, because after a long growing season I'm ready for a slower pace, yet saying goodbye to our beautiful blooms for another year is always sad.

But while the flowers in our fields have faded, heirloom chrysanthemums that have been protected in our greenhouse start to hit their stride, filling the month of November with color once again. The mums, in addition to the heaps of ornamental squash from the garden, bring me incredible joy. What I overlooked during the height of summer now has my full attention: a handful of golden seedpods, a simple bud vase filled with rose hips, or a bowl of heirloom apples collected from a friend's orchard are all treasured. I find myself delighting in all that remains.

Delicate Pastel Statement Piece

Of all the blooms we grow on the farm, dahlias are one of my all-time favorites, second only to sweet peas. Many years ago, when I was just starting out, I got a phone call from my flower-growing mentor Jan Johnson, telling me to load up the kids and my shovel and head over to her house. It was a crisp morning, just after our first hard frost, and she was digging dahlia tubers. I knew very little about dahlias, only that I admired them every time I visited Jan's garden. We worked through the morning, lifting her massive clumps of tubers and splitting off a chunk of each variety for me to take home. Her generosity was my first real taste of just how giving and passionate flower people are. I tried to offer her money or some type of exchange, because she had filled my old station wagon with so many clumps of tubers, but she said she didn't want anything in return, only that I pass along the abundance once my garden was established. From sharing dahlia tubers to teaching me how to make my first bridal bouquet to letting me shadow her during weddings, Jan's support was instrumental in helping me find my way early on.

Since that day, my dahlia garden has grown to include nearly five hundred varieties and over thirteen thousand plants, a far cry from a station wagon full of muddy tubers. While I've grown all colors of the rainbow, it's been a challenge to find varieties in blush tones, though it's one that I'll eagerly accept. Each year I grow dozens of new varieties in search of beauties in this hue to add to the farm's expanding collection, because they are so popular for weddings and event work. Two of my very favorite blush varieties are 'Appleblossom' and 'Break Out'. 'Appleblossom' blooms all summer and into autumn, on medium-size plants that are smothered in perfectly formed petite blooms with glowing golden centers. It's also a favorite with bumblebees, and I have to take great care when harvesting it early in the morning because the bees often sleep in the flowers. 'Break Out' is much less dainty, and its towering plants are equally productive. Both are proven winners here on the farm.

This bouquet celebrates 'Appleblossom' and 'Break Out', which make a stunning pair. One of my favorite colors to combine with blush is chartreuse, so I added mock orange, which turns the most beautiful light apple green as autumn arrives. I also tucked in some frothy clouds of sweet autumn clematis to lend a magical, ephemeral quality, and seedpods for texture. While not obviously eye-catching, sweet Annie and Greek oregano add a delicious herbal scent along with a striking pop of chartreuse, and hydrangeas bring a hint of deeper rose.

INGREDIENTS

Structural foliage
Mock orange (*Philadelphus lewisii*) foliage

Supporting ingredients
Greek oregano seedpods
Hydrangea 'Limelight'
Sweet Annie

Textural ingredients
Lavatera seedpods
Sweet autumn clematis

Supporting flower
Dahlia 'Appleblossom'

Focal flower
Dahlia 'Break Out'

Airy accent
Clematis tangutica 'Bill MacKenzie' seed heads

Clematis
tangutica 'Bill
MacKenzie'
seed heads

Dahlia
'Appleblossom'

Mock orange
(Philadelphus lewisii)
foliage

Lavatera
seedpods

Greek
oregano
seedpods

Sweet
Annie

Hydrangea
'Limelight'

Dahlia
'Break Out'

Sweet
autumn
clematis

Sunset Shades Centerpiece

While leaves are changing everywhere you look, many plants are making seed heads and bearing fruit. These seasonal treasures are among my favorite floral ingredients this time of year.

I've filled our property with as many fruiting plants as I can squeeze in because, along with bearing tasty fruit, they make beautiful bouquet additions. In our vegetable garden we have three long rows of summer fruiting raspberries that provide sturdy green foliage for more than half of the year, from late spring through the first hard frost. We also have two rows of everbearing raspberries that we planted specifically for their long-lasting fruit—they produce two bumper crops, one in early summer and another in early autumn. Blackberries are also a favorite on our farm. Here in Washington state, some kinds of blackberries are invasive and grow wild everywhere. While their fruit is beautiful, the stems of commonly grown types are covered in thick, sharp thorns, so I rarely use them in arrangements. But a few years ago I discovered thornless blackberries, which produce the same beautiful fruit clusters without the prickly stems. Adjacent to the berry patch is our rose garden, which gives us buckets of sweetly scented flowers all summer and beyond, leaving behind exquisite textural rose hips that ripen just in time for late-season arrangements. And along our driveway is a row of 'Evereste' crabapples. This French variety puts on a stellar display of snowy white blooms in the spring, and as soon as the blossoms drop, they are followed by thousands of miniature crabapples that change from green to orange to raspberry as the season progresses. I harvest from these trees every week, but I resist being too greedy so I don't ruin the trees' rounded shapes.

This bouquet celebrates these treasures along with blooms in muted raspberry—one of my favorite color palettes, because it's at once romantic and feminine as well as striking and dramatic. I combined the last of the raspberry-toned dahlias and the first heirloom chrysanthemums with chocolate elderberry foliage and ruby-tinged peony leaves. Among the foliage and flowers, I threaded in all of the best fruiting branches from the garden as a nod to the abundance of the season.

INGREDIENTS

Structural foliage
Elderberry 'Black Beauty'

Supporting ingredients
Dock
Peony foliage
Red-leaf hibiscus 'Mahogany Splendor'
Smokebush 'Grace'
Spirea 'Snowmound' foliage

Textural ingredients
Crabapple 'Evereste'
Everbearing raspberry
Salvia 'Ember's Wish'
Thornless blackberries
Rose hips from 'Windrush' rose

Supporting flowers
Dahlia 'Mystique'
Dahlia 'BJ's Rival'

Focal flowers
Dahlia 'All That Jazz'
Chrysanthemum 'Homecoming'
Dahlia 'Andy's Legacy'
Dahlia 'Vista Minnie'

Airy accents
Rose hips from *Rosa multiflora*
Ornamental grass 'Frosted Explosion'

Dahlia
'All That
Jazz'

Chrysanthemum
'Homecoming'

Salvia
'Ember's
Wish'

Peony
foliage

Elderberry
'Black Beauty'

Red-leaf
hibiscus
'Mahogany
Splendor'

Everbearing
raspberry

Crabapple
'Evereste'

Dahlia
'Andy's
Legacy'

Dock

Dahlia 'Mystique'

Thornless blackberries

Smokebush 'Grace'

Rose hips from 'Windrush' rose

Ornamental grass 'Frosted Explosion'

Dahlia 'BJ's Rival'

Rose hips from *Rosa multiflora*

Dahlia 'Vista Minnie'

Spirea 'Snowmound' foliage

Chrysanthemum Revival Vignette

Chrysanthemums have gotten a bad rap. When I used to deliver blooms to a local flower shop, I often heard discerning customers place bouquet orders and insist that no chrysanthemums be used in their arrangements. The mums they were referring to, and those that are most commonly available, were bred to travel long distances in boxes out of water, and they lack the amazing characteristics that many of their older, lesser-known counterparts have. You will find these standard mums at every big-box store and corner market, often artificially dyed and covered in glitter. It's easy to see why they have fallen out of favor.

It wasn't until I started growing heirloom varieties that I fell madly in love and became a fan for life—and if you can get your hands on them, you will too. Their blooms come in an incredible array of colors, shapes, and forms. Some bloom in tiny little buttons; others are as big as grapefruits. The flowers may be spidery starbursts or have long, cascading petals that look like the feathers of an exotic bird. Not only are the heirloom varieties exquisite, but they also peak at a time of year when most of the garden is going to sleep. I think of them as the last hurrah of the flower season. I am always on the hunt for unique coloring and eye-catching shapes, and chrysanthemums never disappoint. Each year I add a handful of new varieties to our collection of more than a hundred cultivars. This flower family is extremely diverse, and once you become a convert, your collecting may get a bit out of hand.

Although mauve/dusty lavender is not a color I normally associate with this time of year, after walking through the chrysanthemum patch I realized just how many of my favorite varieties fell into this colorway. What was most surprising was the haunting, eerie quality of all of the varieties when displayed together in the retreating autumn light. Arranging them in a vignette is my favorite way to show off these beauties because it allows people to see just how much diversity there can be in a single color within the same family of plants.

INGREDIENTS (ALL FOCAL FLOWERS)

Chrysanthemum 'Savanna Charlton'

Chrysanthemum 'Luxor'

Chrysanthemum 'Lake Landers'

Chrysanthemum 'Kokka Bunmi'

Chrysanthemum 'Pink Fleece'

Chrysanthemum 'Obsession'

Chrysanthemum 'Flair'

Chrysanthemum 'First Light Purple'

Chrysanthemum 'Pink John Wingfield'

Chrysanthemum 'Peter Magnus'

Chrysanthemum 'Norton Vic'

Chrysanthemum 'Bill Holden'

Chrysanthemum 'Lavender Pixie'

Chrysanthemum
'Savanna Charlton'

Chrysanthemum
'Luxor'

Chrysanthemum
'Lake Landers'

Chrysanthemum
'Kokka Bunmi'

Chrysanthemum
'Pink Fleece'

Chrysanthemum
'Obsession'

Chrysanthemum
'Flair'

Chrysanthemum
'Pink John
Wingfield'

Chrysanthemum
'First Light
Purple'

Chrysanthemum
'Peter Magnus'

Chrysanthemum
'Norton Vic'

Chrysanthemum
'Bill Holden'

Chrysanthemum
'Lavender Pixie'

Muted Hues Posy

When I first started growing and arranging flowers, I filled my home library with as many floral design books as I could possibly get my hands on. While most of the titles contained numerous helpful tips and tricks, few of them used flowers that I recognized from my own garden. These books overflowed with contrived creations, including ornately woven grasses and twigs, tightly packed and dome-shaped bouquets, and clear glass vases lined with tropical leaves that were filled with sliced imported fruit; a few even contained pastel candy and miniature marshmallows. The arrangements were definitely unique and innovative, though they had no connection to nature or seasonality. But what struck me most was how garish most of the color combinations were. Each era has its own flavor, and floral designs from the 1990s and early 2000s definitely leaned in the bright, bold direction, with primary colors and screaming jewel tones taking center stage.

By the time I started arranging flowers in earnest, about a decade after most of those books were published, a handful of extremely talented designers—most notably Ariella Chezar, Sarah Ryhanen, Nicolette Owen, Amy Merrick, and Sarah Winward—were paving a new path. These pioneering women highlighted seasonal flowers and worked with subdued, antique color combinations that I had never seen before. Their designs inspired me to think about color in a whole new way and seek out ingredients that had these qualities. I started filling my garden with plants with eerie metallic tones; flowers in muted, muddy colors like chocolate, plum, and soft rose; leaves with mottled coloring and deep veining; plus as many textural, airy ingredients as possible. I sought out and made it my mission to highlight the underdogs of the plant world. Thankfully, this style has taken hold all over the globe, and thousands of floral designers and flower enthusiasts are embracing this softer, more romantic approach to flower arranging.

From late summer into autumn the garden overflows with plants that possess this unusual coloring, and I used some of the most compelling for this posy. One of my all-time favorite flowers to work with this time of year is rudbeckia 'Sahara' because it includes velvety blooms in mixed shades of dusty rose, milk chocolate, copper, rich merlot, and pale lemon. Its hues combine beautifully with ingredients including PeeGee hydrangeas, pokeweed, coppery heuchera leaves, and 'Queen Red Lime' zinnia, which blooms in haunting shades of mossy green, blush, muted coral, and dusty plum.

INGREDIENTS

Structural foliage
Ninebark 'Diablo'

Supporting ingredients
Hydrangea 'Quick Fire'
Heuchera 'Palace Purple'
Oregano 'Hopley's Purple'

Textural ingredients
Celosia Texas Plume Vintage Rose Mix
Pokeweed
Tomato 'Blue Gold Berries'
Autumn fern

Supporting flowers
Zinnia 'Queen Red Lime'
Phlox 'Cherry Caramel'

Focal flower
Black-eyed Susan 'Sahara'

Airy accent
Orach 'Ruby Gold'

Black-eyed Susan 'Sahara'

Hydrangea 'Quick Fire'

Tomato 'Blue Gold Berries'

Celosia Texas Plume Vintage Rose Mix

Orach 'Ruby Gold'

Zinnia 'Queen Red Lime'

Pokeweed

Heuchera
'Palace
Purple'

Autumn
fern

Phlox
'Cherry
Caramel'

Oregano
'Hopley's
Purple'

Ninebark
'Diablo'

Orange and Bronze Hand-Tied Bouquet

When the daylight starts to wane and the nights grow cool, the very first indication that autumn is on its way is that the vine maple, an understory plant here in the Pacific Northwest, starts to change color. This common native grows freely under the forest canopy and is relatively unassuming for most of the year. Only in early autumn does it start to put on a fiery, multicolored display. Each lacy, medium-size plant becomes a psychedelic mix of red, orange, yellow, raspberry, and green, with most leaves containing all of those colors at once. It's not only striking but also lasts incredibly long in the vase. At the same time, the earliest chrysanthemums start flowering, and it's always such a treat to combine them with the last of the dahlias. Similar to the overlap of peonies, garden roses, and ranunculus—which we see as spring transitions into summer—dahlias, mums, and fall foliage collide for an unforgettable late-season display.

When I think of autumn, orange is the first color that comes to mind, and our dahlia patch has more of this hue than any other. As soon as the first frost arrives, the dahlias will be gone for another year, so in this bouquet I combined two gorgeous peachy-orange varieties with some of the earliest changing leaves, miniature rose hips, the first of the mums, and other goodies from the garden that capture the magic of this moment.

INGREDIENTS

Structural foliage
Viburnum 'Popcorn' foliage
Viburnum opulus

Supporting ingredients
Yarrow 'Terracotta'
Vine maple

Textural ingredients
Rose hips
Celosia Texas Plume Summer Sherbet Mix
Gomphrena 'QIS Orange'

Supporting flowers
Dahlia 'Ice Tea'
Chrysanthemum 'Stadium Queen'

Focal flower
Dahlia 'Ferncliff Copper'

Airy accents
Rose hips from *Rosa multiflora*
Northern sea oats

Rose hips
from *Rosa
multiflora*

Northern
sea oats

Yarrow
'Terracotta'

Viburnum
'Popcorn'
foliage

Dahlia
'Ice Tea'

Dahlia
'Ferncliff
Copper'

Rose hips

Gomphrena
'QIS Orange'

Celosia
Texas
Plume
Summer
Sherbet
Mix

*Viburnum
opulus*

Vine maple

Chrysanthemum
'Stadium Queen'

Van Gogh-Inspired En Masse

I have a love-hate relationship with sunflowers. They've long held the top spot as one of the most widely grown cut flowers worldwide, in part because they're extremely easy to grow, are loved by almost everyone, and last forever in a vase. Even if you're a beginning gardener or don't have much space, you can succeed with sunflowers, as they thrive in almost all climates and produce abundantly with very little attention.

But for many years, I spent a full day each week harvesting their heavy, sandpaper-like stems from sunup to sundown for our grocery accounts. I have personally sown, tended, and harvested more than a quarter of a million sunflowers. Although these hardworking customer favorites were the mainstay of our farm for many years, I now grow only small quantities of novelty varieties for flower arranging, and I leave many a flower for pollinators and seed-loving birds.

While the standard golden-petaled, chocolate-centered variety is still the most common, there are dozens of interesting forms and colors to be had, including chocolate, rose, rich ruby red, and ivory. One of my favorite novelty varieties that we grow each year is 'Orange Ruffles'. Its fuzzy dark centers are encircled by pointed shaggy petals that remind me of a lion's mane. I like to arrange sunflowers on their own or with only a few other ingredients because they have such a strong presence and are able to hold their own in a bouquet. Here I've paired 'Orange Ruffles' with airy sprays of miniature flowered *Rudbeckia triloba*, textural bronze fennel, and the dried edible seedpods from the delicious and spicy rat-tail radish. This wild and weedy combination perfectly embraces the end-of-summer slide into autumn.

INGREDIENTS

Structural foliage
Bronze fennel
Dried seedpods from rat-tail radish

Focal flower
Sunflower 'Orange Ruffles'

Airy accent
Black-eyed Susan 'Macau' (*Rudbeckia triloba*)

236

Bronze
fennel

Sunflower
'Orange
Ruffles'

Black-eyed
Susan 'Macau'
(*Rudbeckia
triloba*)

Dried
seedpods
from rat-
tail radish

BONUS TECHNIQUE:
Foraged Wreath

The best thing about autumn wreaths is that they fully embrace the changing season. Unlike their evergreen counterparts, they are not meant to be perfectly formed and lush, and I love having the opportunity to capture the fleeting, tattered, and wild feeling of fall.

Depending on where you live, your foraging choices will vary. You can find many amazing ingredients simply by walking in the woods or cleaning up overgrown corners of your landscape. Be on the lookout for ingredients with interesting textural qualities, unique coloring, or a trailing habit. One of my favorite things to do is squirrel away the best of the wild bits and pieces from the garden as we put it to rest for the season. I find myself rescuing a lot of treasures—including dried seedpods, rose hips, dried hop vines, hydrangea, fruiting branches, and delicate grasses—that are bound for the compost pile, knowing they will look amazing in my creations. Autumn leaves look spectacular in a wreath, but few varieties hold their color after being cut. Copper beech and oak leaves are two of the longest-lasting and best options if you want to incorporate foliage into your wreath.

On the East Coast of the United States, grapes grow wild the way blackberries do here in the Northwest, and their long, gnarled vines make a perfect base for autumn wreaths. We grow grapes for eating in our garden and have an abundance of left-over vines to work with after we've harvested the fruit. The best part of using a grapevine base is that they never make a perfect circle. The whimsical, imperfect shape guides the direction and overall aesthetic of the finished wreath. I love the craggy, gnarled wood and curlicues so much that I often leave part of the grape-vine exposed because it adds so much texture and character. If you don't have grapevines readily available, young willow, filbert, or dogwood branches are great alternatives as long as they are freshly cut and pliable.

TO MAKE A FORAGED WREATH, YOU WILL NEED:

Supplies

Oasis waterproof tape

Paddle wire

Snips

Ingredients

Seven 6 to 8 ft (2 to 2.5 m) grapevines with foliage removed

Twelve 10 to 24 in (25 to 61 cm) stems copper beech

Seven 12 to 36 in (30 to 91 cm) hop vines

Seven 6 to 9 in (15 to 23 cm) stems rose hips from rose 'James Galway'

Five 4 to 6 in (10 to 15 cm) stems rose hips from *Rosa dupontii*

Six 6 to 9 in (15 to 23 cm) stems echinacea 'Magnus' seed heads

Five 12 to 17 in (30 to 43 cm) stems northern sea oats

241

1. Create the base by gathering 4 lengths of grapevines and forming them into a circle, weaving the ends around the base once or twice to maintain the shape.

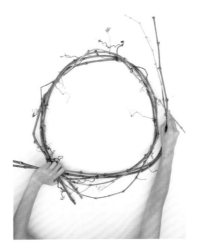

2. Holding the circle in one hand, take the remaining 3 lengths of grapevines and weave them in the opposite direction, again wrapping the ends around the base multiple times for added strength.

3. Secure the shape by wrapping a piece of waterproof tape around the vines where the ends meet.

4. Place the copper beech stems in a crescent shape on the lower portion of the circle and secure in place with paddle wire.

5. Gently wrap the dried hop vines around the entire base.

6. Poke the rose hips into the gaps between vines all around the wreath.

7. Tuck the echinacea seed heads into the gaps in the base.

8. Thread in the delicate sea oat stems or more hops for additional texture.

Winter

Our farm is situated in the northernmost part of Washington, about an hour south of the Canadian border. Our winters are long, dark, and extremely wet, and a thick layer of gray clouds and fog usually blankets the sky. During the darkest months, the sun sets by midafternoon, and it's hard to find motivation to do anything but dream of warmer days ahead. Thankfully, the garden catalogs start pouring in around the first of the year, and with them the promise of flowers just over the horizon.

This time of year our garden is bare, and the once-lush hedgerows and perennial borders that surround our property are merely skeletons in the landscape. On sunny days, all of the songbirds that make their home on our land appear by the thousands, scrounging for fallen seeds and berries. Blooms that went unpicked during the growing season have become textural pods that look striking on frozen mornings, like they've been dusted with glitter. I like to leave them in place to provide a cold-weather food source for the birds.

Winter is the one season when I let myself buy as many flowers as I want. I steer clear of imported blooms, and instead seek out spring-flowering bulbs that have been forced indoors—which means they've been coaxed to bloom outside their usual season—by local growers. Tulips, paperwhites, amaryllis, and hyacinths are easy to find nearby and provide a much-needed flower fix to get me through the bleak months. We're lucky to have one of the last domestic rose growers just a few hours south of us, and their garden roses and lilies are the ultimate treat in these cold months. Unlike the other seasons, when there is an abundant selection of foliage and textural ingredients, during the lean months of winter I find myself dipping into my dried flower stash and foraging heavily in search of the unexpected.

247

Snowy White Statement Piece

Although evergreens grow wild everywhere in the Pacific Northwest, the only time I find myself really using them in arrangements is during winter. In any other time of the year they seem out of place. While the rich emerald greens are most commonly associated with the holidays, I've found that some of the more architectural and uniquely colored silver options are quite versatile and add a refreshing twist to winter arrangements.

With stately evergreens creating a dramatic framework, focal flowers need to be equally showstopping, and it's not often that you have the opportunity to incorporate large, unexpected blooms such as flowering kale, amaryllis, and flower-like poinsettia bracts. I chose them in white—it's one of the best colors to display on its own against an evergreen backdrop—and I continually find myself coming back to this no-fail monochromatic palette, especially when ingredients are more limited than usual. All three of these massive beauties last an incredibly long time in the vase but need a little special treatment to keep their staying power, so be sure to refer to the "A–Z Ingredient Guide" (page 282).

I built this arrangement in a large vintage sap bucket that my friend Nina brought to me from Vermont. Its weight and stature are perfect for supporting the heavy Atlas cedar and cypress branches. We are lucky to live next to a farm that specializes in winter vegetables, and they gave me permission to harvest full stalks of lacinato kale, which add a rich textural quality to the mix. To add sparkle, I tucked in delicate wands of dried Russian sage and a few clusters of native snowberries that had been left by the birds. One of my favorite things about this arrangement was how long it lasted. By placing it in a cool room and refilling the water regularly, I was able to enjoy it for two glorious weeks.

INGREDIENTS

Structural foliage
Atlas cedar
Cypress 'Silver Smoke'
Cedar 'Glauca Pendula'

Supporting ingredients
Poinsettia 'Whitestar'
Flowering kale 'Flare White'
Kale 'Lacinato'

Textural ingredients
Snowberry
Saucer magnolia branches

Supporting flowers
Nerine 'Stephanie'
Chrysanthemum, unknown variety

Focal flower
Amaryllis 'Snow White'

Airy accents
Clematis 'Bill MacKenzie' seed heads
Russian sage bracts

248

Nerine
'Stephanie'

Clematis
'Bill
MacKenzie'
seed heads

Atlas
cedar

Snowberry

Amaryllis
'Snow White'

Cypress
'Silver
Smoke'

Flowering kale
'Flare White'

Saucer
magnolia
branches

Kale
'Lacinato'

Poinsettia
'Whitestar'

Russian
sage
bracts

Cedar
'Glauca
Pendula'

Chrysanthemum,
unknown variety

Peach and Bronze Centerpiece

One of my favorite ways to round out what's available for winter arrangements is to incorporate ingredients that we've dried from the summer harvest—some of the best materials to preserve this way are strawflower, statice, globe amaranth (gomphrena), larkspur, and cress. Drying flowers is easy: just pick them when they are fully open but not overly ripe and hang them upside down in a warm, dry place for a few weeks until they are firm and completely dry. Then you can gently wrap dried bundles in newspaper and store them away until winter, when they come in handy for wreath making, dried crafts, and weaving in with fresh flowers. Dried material is quite fragile, so handle it with care.

With dried ingredients, I mix in some fresh surprises, including garden roses, which I love treating myself to as we usher in the new year. I especially love the ones from Peterkort Roses, since they grow year round and are just a few hours south of our farm. I first discovered Peterkort when I was seeking a local rose source. The wholesale farm near Portland, Oregon, has been family owned and operated since 1923. In their sixteen greenhouses, spanning more than six acres, they grow over a hundred thousand rose plants along with thousands of lilies, freesias, orchids, and maidenhair ferns. In the past decade, I don't think we've done a single wedding that hasn't included at least a few stems of Peterkort roses. Everything they grow is magical and of the highest quality.

For this arrangement, I chose one of my favorite terra-cotta footed bowls from Campo de' Fiori, then scoured our property for unexpected ingredients. I created a base using chocolatey azalea foliage, maroon pieris buds, and an unusual copper yew to set off large peach amaryllis that were left over from the holidays. Dried strawflowers and fragrant hyacinths accentuate the amaryllises' soft color, and beautiful, creamy peach spray roses from Peterkort add softness. I saved the most delicate ingredients for last, threading in a few stems of dried cress and fuzzy golden grasses for movement and sparkle. I love how beautiful and romantic this centerpiece turned out, given the time of year.

INGREDIENTS

Structural foliage
Azalea foliage, unknown variety

Supporting ingredient
Hicks yew

Textural ingredients
Pieris buds
Pepper tree berries

Supporting flowers
Strawflower Silvery Rose
Hyacinth 'Gypsy Queen'
Rose 'Princess Bride'

Focal flower
Amaryllis 'Peach Melba'

Airy accents
Ornamental grass 'Bunny Tails' (dried)
Cress 'Wrinkled Crinkled' (dried)

254

Pieris buds

Ornamental grass
'Bunny Tails'
(dried)

Pepper tree
berries

Azalea
foliage,
unknown
variety

Amaryllis
'Peach Melba'

Strawflower
Silvery Rose

Hyacinth
'Gypsy Queen'

Cress
'Wrinkled
Crinkled'
(dried)

Hicks yew

Rose
'Princess
Bride'

A Study in Red Vignette

When we first started hosting on-farm design workshops, we had no idea how many amazing people would make the trip to learn about seasonally based floral design. One of the most surprising attendees was famed East Coast potter Frances Palmer, who came to our peony-focused workshop. Frances is among the most celebrated ceramic artists in the United States; her work has been featured in countless books, magazines, and articles. The first morning of that workshop, I was beyond nervous knowing that such a talented and well-respected artist would be in our midst. Little did I know that I had nothing to fear: Frances exudes warmth and quickly had the entire class madly in love with her.

In addition to being a talented ceramicist, Frances is also a gifted flower arranger. She shares the most beautiful photos on social media, and the scenes she creates with seasonal blooms in her stunning pottery always inspire me. Over the years, I have been gradually collecting her work, adding one precious piece at a time, and I now have a full shelf devoted to these exquisite and delicate works of art.

One of the easiest and most striking ways to decorate for the holidays is to line a table with interesting vessels filled with several ingredients, all in the same color. Red is such a rich, saturated hue that it can easily carry a display on its own, so for this grouping I arranged red varieties in some of my treasured Frances Palmer pottery. I intentionally kept the blooms simple, using just one type per vase, so the vessels and the jewel-like quality of the flowers would take center stage. The effect is dramatic and couldn't be easier, taking less than ten minutes to create.

INGREDIENTS (ALL FOCAL FLOWERS)

Amaryllis 'Red Lion'

Holly with leaves removed

Rose 'Piano'

Poinsettia 'Astro Red'

Nerine 'Red Robin'

Nerine
'Red Robin'

Amaryllis
'Red Lion'

Holly
with
leaves
removed

Rose
'Piano'

Poinsettia
'Astro Red'

Rose and Plum Posy

As winter draws to a close, my longing for flowers reaches its all-time peak. I spend a good part of my days planning for the season ahead, and I walk the garden daily looking for signs of life. Every bloom is treasured at this time of year, and I find myself picking even the shortest stems to display in tiny vases throughout the house.

One of the first flowers to emerge in the new year is the hellebore. Commonly called Lenten roses, hellebores are super easy to grow and extremely long-lived. These little beauties bloom from mid- to late winter all the way through early summer. They come in a gorgeous array of colors, including pink, mauve, an almost-black burgundy, green, buttery yellow, and creamy whites. Some of my favorites include those with frilly double and delicately freckled blossoms. Hellebores thrive in the shade, so they're a great choice if your garden doesn't have full sun. Their rough, serrated leaves also make them resistant to deer and other critters.

For this posy, I used a base of ruffled purple kale—a wonderful winter foliage option for arrangements. Dark pieris buds and nandina foliage echo the kale's rich, moody hue. I normally use hellebores as a supporting ingredient, but for this petite arrangement they take center stage. A poinsettia left over from the holidays has layers of tones that add brightness and muted coloring to complement the hellebores. This sweet little bouquet helped carry me through a long stretch of planning and the last few days of winter.

INGREDIENTS

Structural foliage
Kale 'Redbor'

Supporting ingredients
Pieris buds
Viburnum tinus 'Spring Bouquet'

Textural ingredient
Pepper tree berries

Supporting flower
Poinsettia 'Freedom Marble'

Focal flower
Hellebore Ivory Prince

Airy accent
Nandina foliage

264

Pieris
buds

Kale
'Redbor'

Nandina
foliage

Poinsettia
'Freedom
Marble'

Hellebore
Ivory
Prince

Viburnum
tinus
'Spring
Bouquet'

Pepper tree
berries

Black and White Bridal Bouquet

When the fields are overflowing with flowers during the warmer seasons, bridal bouquets come together almost effortlessly. A quick stroll through the field or a visit to the local flower market provides ample inspiration and a bounty of material to work with. But once winter arrives, you have to work a whole lot harder.

Over the many years that we designed flowers for weddings, I did only a handful of winter events. Because our design studio was committed to sourcing seasonal flowers grown as close to home as possible, supplying weddings in the coldest months proved to be tricky. It was even harder when the couple had a complicated color palette or their hearts set on specific varieties that had to be flown in from halfway across the world. Every time a bride would write to me about her winter nuptials, I would try my best to refer her to another florist who used more imported blooms.

But it is possible to create beautiful wedding bouquets using locally sourced flowers, even in the dead of winter. Some growers force bulbs such as ranunculus, tulips, hyacinths, anemones, and paperwhites, making them relatively easy to find. It's important to note that bulb flowers are quite fragile and break easily, so you must take great care when working with them. For this bouquet, I combined some of the very best bulb flowers I could get my hands on and paired them with privet berries from our hedgerows, rose-scented geraniums from our greenhouse, and the tiniest tips of hemlock for a lacy effect. The dark purple-black berries of the privet help accentuate the dark eyes of the anemones, and the hyacinths and paperwhites infuse the bouquet with a heady aroma that makes it impossible to put down.

INGREDIENTS

Structural foliage
Boxwood tips

Supporting ingredient
Scented geranium 'Attar of Roses'

Textural ingredients
Berries from Chinese privet (*Ligustrum sinense*)
Berries from European privet (*Ligustrum vulgare*)

Supporting flowers
Hyacinth 'White Pearl'
Tulip 'Honeymoon'
Tulip 'Rialto'
Paperwhite 'Ziva' (*Narcissus*)

Focal flowers
Anemone 'Galilee Black and White'
Ranunculus 'La Belle White'

Airy accent
Hemlock tips

Tulip
'Honeymoon'

Berries from
Chinese privet
(*Ligustrum
sinense*)

Boxwood
tips

Hyacinth
'White
Pearl'

Tulip
'Rialto'

Paperwhite
'Ziva'
(*Narcissus*)

Scented
geranium
'Attar of
Roses'

Ranunculus
'La Belle
White'

Berries
from
European
privet (*Ligustrum
vulgare*)

Hemlock
tips

Anemone
'Galilee
Black and
White'

Winter Light En Masse

There are few things more luxurious than a heaving bunch of 'Casa Blanca' lilies. Each tall waxy stem bears three to five green buds that are quite unassuming when closed, but as they open they grow in both size and grandeur, unfurling into perfect snow-white petals. 'Casa Blanca' is an Oriental-type lily, and one stem of these towering beauties offers enough fragrance to fill an entire room. People either love the fragrance or are completely revolted by it. I personally adore their sweet, sugary scent that seems to hang in the air.

Oriental lilies bloom in the garden in midsummer but are often locally grown in heated greenhouses throughout the winter months, and bringing home a bundle of them for special occasions always feels like a decadent treat. Lilies are an extremely long-lasting cut flower; I find that they generally persist for up to ten days in the vase, opening slowly over time. Lily pollen can easily stain clothing and furniture, so as soon as the blooms crack open, use a piece of tissue to gently pull off the brown pollen anthers before they turn orange and fuzzy. Once the blooms open they become much harder to transport and their petals will bruise and break easily, so when buying lilies, choose stems that are still in bud and arrange them before the buds open.

I think that lilies are best displayed on their own, as their large flowers are difficult to incorporate into mixed arrangements. Given the right vessel and room to unfurl, an arrangement of these is simply stunning. For this arrangement, I used a base of airy filbert branches with chartreuse catkins in a Farmhouse Pottery crock to add a little sparkle. I then carefully threaded in the lily stems around the perimeter of the vase, leaving the tallest stems in the middle, then added river birch catkins for an additional dash of texture.

INGREDIENTS

Textural ingredients
Filbert
River birch catkins

Focal flower
'Casa Blanca' lily

274

River
birch
catkins

Filbert

'Casa
Blanca'
lily

BONUS TECHNIQUE:
Evergreen Wreath

My favorite way to usher in the holiday season is by making a big batch of evergreen wreaths and garlands. They are easy to assemble and extremely long lasting, and they make fantastic gifts for family and friends. The best part is that you can scrounge all of the material from the garden or forage locally (with permission when needed) for free. In Washington, late fall and early winter are usually pretty stormy, and after a heavy windstorm there are branches for the taking everywhere. I just drive up and down the back roads and can fill the entire bed of our pickup truck in less than an hour. Looking for ingredients always feels like a treasure hunt.

The Pacific Northwest is known for its towering evergreens, and every hillside, mountain, and public space is home to so many different species of conifers. I normally take the abundance for granted, but in the winter months I find myself wanting to highlight these native treasures. There is no shortage of material to work with.

When making wreaths, after I gather a selection of evergreens, I spend time hunting for the accent greens and textural pieces that will make each finished wreath pop. Berries, ivy, ferns, branches with catkins, and seedpods are all favorites. This wild, textural wreath is an ode to the Pacific Northwest, featuring many varieties that are native to our neck of the woods.

TO MAKE AN EVERGREEN WREATH, YOU WILL NEED:

Supplies

12 in (30 cm) diameter wreath frame

Spool of floral wire

Heavy-duty clippers

Wide variety of evergreen foliage and textural ingredients

Ingredients

48 to 60 stems assorted evergreens cut down to 6 to 8 in (15 to 20 cm) lengths

Eight 8 in (20 cm) sprigs holly

Six 6 to 8 in (15 to 20 cm) boxwood sprigs

Eighteen 6 to 8 in (15 to 20 cm) fern tips

Thirteen 12 to 15 in (30 to 38 cm) ivy vines

10 sprigs ivy berries

279

1. Lay out the wreath frame, wire, and clippers. This metal ring came from a craft store, but you can also make your own wreath base from grapevines (see "Foraged Wreath" on page 241).

2. Make 12 to 15 mixed evergreen bundles, using about 4 stems per bundle. These will become the foundation of your wreath. Place the more basic evergreens at the back of the bundle and the more unique ingredients at the front.

280

3. Lay one bundle of greens on your wreath frame and secure it in place with a few wraps of floral wire.

4. Place the next bundle a few inches away on the frame, with the greenery facing in the same direction as the first, and secure it to the frame with wire.

5. Continue adding bundles and wiring them down, covering the entire frame in greens.

6. Once the base of the wreath is complete, insert ingredients that you want to stand out. I tucked in sprigs of holly and boxwood evenly around the wreath.

7. Layer in embellishments that you want to highlight. I wrapped ivy vines around the evergreen base and in between the holly sprigs.

8. Add any special touches that will really make your finished wreath pop. I poked fern tips and ivy berries among the holly and ivy vines for texture and interest.

A-Z Ingredient Guide

The following are ingredients shown in the book's projects along with additional favorites you may want to create with. For each, you'll see how long you can expect it to last after being cut and any special harvesting and care tips.

Some ingredients may also include a notation that the plant is dirty, sappy, wimpy, or woody. This indicates that it requires special treatment for greatest longevity—see "Hydration Categories" on page 36 for treatment guidelines, along with what's detailed here.

Akebia
Vase Life: 6 to 8 days

Harvest vines as soon as blooms appear, or cut older, woodier stems for foliage. **Woody.**

Allium
Vase Life: 14+ days

Harvest when 50 percent of the florets are open. Flowers can be stored for up to one month in the cooler if you use holding solution. Seed heads can also be dried.

Amaranth
Vase Life: 7 to 10 days

Harvest upright varieties when seed heads are three-quarters open. Harvest cascading varieties when tassels begin to elongate. Remove foliage so spikes and tassels are more visible.

Amaryllis (*Hippeastrum* species)
Vase Life: 14+ days

Harvest when flowers are in bud and showing color. Use care, as buds bruise easily. To prevent stems from collapsing under their own weight, slip a long, thin bamboo skewer through the hollow stem; secure with a cotton ball.

Anemone
Vase Life: 7 to 10 days

Harvest when buds are fully colored.

Angelica
Vase Life: 7 to 10 days

Harvest when the primary flower umbel is open and side blooms are starting to open, or let the umbel develop and pick after the seedpods mature.

Apple of Peru (*Nicandra physalodes*)
Vase Life: 7 days

Harvest once seedpods have formed, removing foliage so the lanterns are more visible.

Artemisia
Vase Life: 5 to 7 days

Harvest once stems have become firm and are no longer floppy when wiggled. Strip the lower third of foliage. Dry by hanging them upside down in a warm, dark place for 2 to 3 weeks. **Wimpy.**

Astilbe
Vase Life: 4 to 10 days

Harvest when one-half to three-quarters of the flowers are open and the uppermost buds are swollen and showing color. Immediately place cut stems in water. Astilbe is extremely ethylene sensitive; keep away from ripening fruit.

Azalea
Vase Life: 7+ days

Harvest when half of the blooms in a cluster are open for flowers. For foliage, harvest once leaves are leathery and firm. **Woody.**

Baby's breath (*Gypsophila* species)
Vase Life: 5 to 10 days

Harvest when 60 percent of the flowers on a stem are open.

Bachelor's button (*Centaurea cyanus*)
Vase Life: 6 to 10 days

Harvest when blooms are one-quarter to one-half open. If picking entire sprays, cut when half the flowers on a spray are open.

Basil (*Ocimum basilicum*)
Vase Life: 7 to 10 days

Harvest when stems begin to toughen, or as soon as flowers begin to form. It's especially wilt prone, so be sure to cut during the coolest part of the day to minimize wilting. Do not put into the cooler or the foliage will turn black. **Wimpy.**

Bee balm (*Monarda hybrida*)
Vase Life: 7 to 10 days

Harvest when flower whorls begin to turn from green to purple. It's especially wilt prone, so be sure to cut during the coolest part of the day to minimize wilting. **Wimpy.**

Beech (*Fagus sylvatica*)
Vase Life: 14 days

Harvest when foliage becomes leathery to the touch. After stems have been conditioned, beech can be used out of water for arbors and garlands. **Woody.**

Bells of Ireland (*Moluccella laevis*)

Vase Life: 7 to 10 days

Harvest once the green bells start to form along the stem; remove leaves from the lower half of the stem, as they will yellow prematurely.

Birch (*Betula* species)

Vase Life: 7 to 10 days

Harvest branches when leaves have dropped and catkins have swelled. Cut before yellow pollen appears.

Bittersweet (*Celastrus scandens*)

Vase Life: 14+ days

Harvest when fruit pods are greenish-yellow, and remove all foliage. Cut before pods have popped opened, or they will shatter when handled. Can also be dried. **Woody.**

Blackberry

Vase Life: 5 to 7 days

Harvest when fruit is fully colored and still shiny. For foliage, harvest when leaves have become leathery and firm.

Black-eyed Susan (*Rudbeckia* species)

Vase Life: 7 to 10 days

Harvest when flowers are just beginning to open. **Dirty.**

Bleeding heart (*Lamprocapnos spectabilis*)

Vase Life: 7 days

Harvest when 3 to 5 flowers on a stem have opened.

Blue bells (*Scilla siberica*)

Vase Life: 7 to 10 days

Harvest when flowers are half open.

Blueberry (*Vaccinium* species)

Vase Life: 7 to 14 days

Harvest when foliage has become leathery and firm and before fruit begins to color.

Boxwood (*Buxus* species)

Vase Life: 3 to 5 weeks

Harvest firm, woody stems at desired length. May have an unpleasant odor. **Woody.**

Bupleurum

Vase Life: 8 to 10 days

Harvest when flowers are fully open to avoid wilting.

Calendula

Vase Life: 6 to 8 days

Harvest when flowers are three-quarters open. Foliage is sticky, so wear gloves when harvesting.

California poppy (*Eschscholzia californica*)

Vase Life: 3 to 4 days

Harvest when flowers are in colored bud stage. As old flowers fade and drop petals, new buds on the stem pop open, giving you at least a week's worth of flowers.

Camellia

Vase Life: 5 to 10 days

Harvest when flower buds are just opening. For foliage, harvest when leaves are leathery and stems are firm. Woody.

Campion (*Silene* species)

Vase Life: 7 days

Harvest as soon as flowers begin to open on a stem.

Candytuft (*Iberis amara*)

Vase Life: 7 days

Harvest when one-quarter to one-third of the florets on a stem are open. A beautiful, early airy filler, but has an unpleasant smell. Seed heads can be dried and used indefinitely.

Canterbury bells (*Campanula medium*)

Vase Life: 10 to 14 days

Harvest when just a few flowers are open on a stem.

Cape fuchsia (*Phygelius* species)

Vase Life: 7 to 10 days

Harvest when one-third of the flowers on a stem are open.

Carnation (*Dianthus caryophyllus*)

Vase Life: Up to 14 days

Harvest when 1 or 2 flowers on a spray are open.

Celosia

Vase Life: 10 to 14 days

Harvest once flower heads reach desired size, but before they go to seed. Strip 80 percent of the foliage off during harvest. Do not put into the cooler.

China aster (*Callistephus chinensis*)

Vase Life: 7 to 10 days

Harvest single-stemmed varieties when flowers are 50 percent open. For spray varieties, harvest when one-quarter of the flowers on a stem have opened.

Chinese lantern (*Physalis alkekengi*)

Vase Life: 2+ weeks

Harvest when pods have changed to orange, cutting stems off at ground level and removing all foliage. Dry by hanging upside down in a warm, dark place for 2 to 3 weeks.

Chocolate Queen Anne's Lace (*Daucus carota*)

Vase Life: 6 to 8 days

Harvest when flowers have fully opened and lie flat, otherwise stems tend to wilt.

Chrysanthemum

Vase Life: 14+ days

Harvest individual stems when the flowers are one-half to two-thirds open. For spray varieties, harvest when one-quarter of the flowers on a stem have opened. Dirty.

Clematis

Vase Life: 7 days

Harvest blooms when one-quarter of flowers on a stem have opened. For foliage, harvest when stems and leaves become leathery. Wimpy.

Clover

Vase Life: 5 to 7 days

Harvest when flowers are one-half to two-thirds of the way open.

Columbine (*Aquilegia* species)

Vase Life: 6 to 8 days

Harvest when one-third of flowers on the stem have opened, and before any begin to drop their petals.

Corn cockle (*Agrostemma githago*)

Vase Life: 5 to 7 days

Harvest when 1 or 2 flowers on a stem are open. Wimpy.

Cosmos

Vase Life: 5 to 6 days

Harvest when buds are just cracking, but haven't fully opened. For double varieties, let open halfway before picking.

Crabapple

Vase Life: 7 days

Harvest blooms when one-quarter of flowers are open on the stem, and strip the bottom third of foliage. Harvest fruit at desired size, and remove most of the foliage. For foliage, harvest when leaves are leathery. Woody.

Cress (*Lepidium sativum*)

Vase Life: 7 to 10 days

Harvest when seedpods are fully formed and the top blooms have faded. Seed heads can be dried and used indefinitely.

Cup-and-saucer vine (*Cobaea scandens*)

Vase Life: 4 to 5 days

Harvest individual flowers just as they open. Wimpy.

Dahlia

Vase Life: 5 days

Cut when blooms are three-quarters of the way open. It's especially important to put them into water with hydration solution, or place in very hot water, just off boiling, and leave in the water as it cools for one hour.

Delphinium

Vase Life: 7 to 9 days

Harvest when bottom one-third of flowers on the stem are open. Delphinium is extremely ethylene sensitive; keep away from ripening fruit.

Deutzia

Vase Life: 4 to 6 days

Harvest when buds are swollen or flowers have just begun to open.

Dill (*Anethum graveolens*)

Vase Life: 7 to 10 days

Harvest when flower heads are fully developed and bright yellow. Seed heads can also be dried and used indefinitely.

Dock (*Rumex species*)

Vase Life: 7 to 10 days

Harvest once seedpods have formed on the stem.

Dusty miller (*Senecio cineraria*)
Vase Life: 7 to 10 days

Harvest when stems are mature and firm. Foliage is especially wilt prone, so be sure to harvest during the coolest part of the day. Wimpy.

Echinacea
Vase Life: 7 to 10 days

Harvest flowers when outer petals are emerging around the cone. Harvest cones while still fully intact and remove outer petals. To dry cones, remove all petals and hang stems upside down in a warm, dark place for 2 to 3 weeks.

Elaeagnus
Vase Life: 14+ days

Harvest once leaves have become leathery. Elaeagnus can be used out of water for arbors and garlands.

Elderberry (*Sambucus nigra*)
Vase Life: 5 to 7 days

Harvest when foliage is leathery. Foliage has a smoky, unpleasant odor. Use Quick Dip and place into water with hydration solution. Woody.

Eucalyptus
Vase Life: 14+ days

Harvest once foliage is mature and tips are no longer droopy. Can also be dried and used indefinitely.

Euphorbia
Vase Life: 7 to 10 days

Harvest when flowers are fully colored but not completely open. Use caution and wear gloves when harvesting, as the sap is irritating to the skin and eyes. Sappy.

European hornbeam (*Carpinus betulus*)
Vase Life: 14+ days

Harvest when foliage is leathery to the touch. After stems have been conditioned, hornbeam can be used out of water for arbors and garlands. Woody.

Evergreens (includes cedar, cypress, fir, hemlock, juniper, pine, spruce, and yew)
Vase Life: 14+ days

Harvest mature foliage. Can be used out of water.

False Queen Anne's lace (*Ammi majus, A. visnaga*)
Vase Life: 6 to 8 days

Pick when 80 percent of the flowers on a stem are open. Stems tend to wilt if harvested earlier. Can cause skin irritation, so wear long sleeves and gloves when harvesting.

Fennel (*Foeniculum vulgare*)
Vase Life: 7 to 10 days

Harvest when flower heads are fully developed. Seed heads can also be dried and used indefinitely.

Fern
Vase Life: 7+ days

Harvest fronds once leaves are leathery to the touch and tips are fully unfurled.

Feverfew (*Tanacetum parthenium*)
Vase Life: 7 to 10 days

Harvest when one-quarter to one-half of the flowers on a spray are open.

Filbert (*Corylus* species)
Vase Life: 7 to 10 days

Harvest branches when leaves have dropped and catkins have swelled. Cut before yellow pollen appears. **Woody.**

Filipendula (*Filipendula ulmaria*)
Vase Life: 7 days

Harvest when three-quarters of the florets are open.

Flax (*Linum usitatissimum*)
Vase Life: 10 days

Harvest after the flowers drop their petals and leave behind their seedpods. Over time, the green pods fade to gold and can be dried.

Flowering branches (includes trees that bloom in spring, such as apple, cherry, and hawthorn)
Vase Life: 7 days

Harvest blooms when one-quarter of flowers are open on the stem. Strip the bottom third of foliage. **Woody.**

Flowering tobacco (*Nicotiana* species)
Vase Life: 7 days

Harvest when one-third of flowers are open on a stem. Flowers are especially wilt prone, so always harvest during the coolest part of the day. **Wimpy.**

Forget-me-not
Vase Life: 5 to 7 days

Harvest when one-quarter of the flowers on a stem are open. It's especially wilt prone, so be sure to cut during the coolest part of the day. **Wimpy.**

Forsythia (*Forsythia × intermedia*)
Vase Life: 7 to 14 days

For flowers, harvest stems when buds start to swell. For foliage, pick once leaves are mature. Forsythia foliage is a long-lasting cut (up to 2 weeks) if picked after it has firmed up and feels leathery. **Woody.**

Foxglove (*Digitalis purpurea*)
Vase Life: 6 to 8 days

Harvest when just a few bottom blossoms are open, before the bees pollinate the flowers.

Freesia
Vase Life: 7 days

Harvest when 1 or 2 flowers on a stem are open. Freesia is extremely ethylene sensitive; keep away from ripening fruit.

Fritillaria
Vase Life: 6 to 7 days

Harvest when one-half to three-quarters of the blossoms are open.

Geranium
Vase Life: 5 days

Harvest when flowers are just starting to open.

Geum
Vase Life: 7 days

Harvest when one-quarter to one-half of flowers on a stem have opened.

Gladiolus
Vase Life: 7 to 10 days

Harvest when the bottom 2 to 5 blossoms on a spike are in colored bud.

Globe thistle (*Echinops*)
Vase Life: 7 to 10 days

Harvest when a majority of the globe has turned blue, but before the flower petals begin to form. Foliage will yellow prematurely, so remove at harvest.

Goat's beard (*Aruncus dioicus*)
Vase Life: 7 to 10 days

Harvest flowers when one-half to three-quarters of the florets are open.

Godetia (*Clarkia amoena*)
Vase Life: 7 days

Harvest when the first blossom on each stem opens. Although individual flowers only last a handful of days, they are quickly replaced with new blooms.

Gomphrena
Vase Life: 14+ days

Harvest when the flowers have colored up and stems are firm. To dry flowers, let them open completely and hang upside down in a warm, dark place for a few weeks.

Grains (including barley, oats, and rye)
Vase Life: 7 to 10 days

Harvest when seed heads are large and fully formed, and any top blooms have faded. Remove most of the foliage. To dry, harvest after blooms have dropped their pollen, and hang bundles upside down in a warm, dry, dark place.

Grape hyacinth (*Muscari azureum*)
Vase Life: 7 days

Harvest when one-third to one-half of the florets are open.

Grapes (*Vitis vinifera*)
Vase Life: 7 days or indefinite if vines are used for wreaths

For fruit, harvest before the cluster is showing much color. For foliage, harvest once leaves are leathery and stems are firm.

Grasses
Vase Life: 7+ days

Seed heads should be harvested as soon as they emerge, or after the pollen has shed.

Hellebore
Vase Life: 5 to 7 days

Harvest after the flower stamens are gone and seeds have begun to form. The more developed the seedpods, the sturdier and longer lasting the cut hellebore will be. **Wimpy.**

Heuchera
Vase Life: 7 to 10 days

For flowers, harvest when half the florets on a stem are open. For foliage, cut leaf stems at ground level for the longest stems.

Holly (*Ilex species*)
Vase Life: 14+ days

Harvest foliage at any time. Harvest fruit when green or fully colored.

Honeysuckle (*Lonicera* species)
Vase Life: 7 to 10 days

For flowers, harvest before buds open. For foliage, harvest once leaves are fully mature and strip off lower leaves. For vines, harvest as soon as blooms appear, or cut older, woodier stems for foliage; strip off lower leaves. **Woody.**

Honeywort (*Cerinthe major*)
Vase Life: 7 to 10 days

Harvest once flowers are fully formed on arched stems, but before seeds start to form. It's especially wilt prone, so cut during the coolest part of the day. **Wimpy.**

Hops (*Humulus lupulus*)
Vase Life: 7 days

Harvest any time after flower bracts have formed; remove leaves for best display. Foliage is scratchy, so wear gloves and long sleeves when harvesting.

Hyacinth
Vase Life: 7 days

Harvest when one-third to one-half of the lower blossoms are open. Can be stored out of water in a cooler for 1 week with the bulb on. Remove the bulb when ready to display.

Hyacinth bean (*Dolichos lablab*)
Vase Life: 7 to 10 days

Harvest when the purple beans have fully formed.

Hydrangea
Vase Life: 7 to 10 days

Harvest when the flowers are completely open, and remove most of the foliage. **Woody.**

Hypericum
Vase Life: 14+ days

Harvest when the fruit begins to turn color, cutting long stems.

Iceland poppy (*Papaver nudicaule*)
Vase Life: 5 to 7 days

Harvest when buds are just starting to crack open. Once the flowers open fully, they're prone to damage. The boiling water dip is more effective than Quick Dip. **Wimpy.**

Iris (*Iris × germanica*)
Vase Life: 3 to 7 days

Harvest when flower buds have fully emerged from green sheaths and are showing color. Remove faded flowers, and buds will continue to emerge.

Ivy (*Hedera* species)

Vase Life: 7 to 10 days

Harvest sturdy vines in long sections at any time of the year. Mature vines produce black berries that can also be used for arrangements.

Japanese anemone (*Anemone hupehensis* var. *japonica*)

Vase Life: 7 days

Pick when one-quarter of the flowers on a stem have opened. As older blooms fade, new ones appear.

Kale (includes ornamental cabbage/ kale and edible kale)

Vase Life: 14 days

For flowering types, harvest when flower heads resemble a rose blossom. Remove all of the lower leaves. For edible kale, harvest at desired size. Dirty.

Lady's mantle (*Alchemilla mollis*)

Vase Life: 7 to 10 days

Harvest when three-quarters of the flowers on a stem are open.

Larkspur (*Delphinium consolida*)

Vase Life: 5 to 7 days

Harvest when one-third of the blossoms are open on a stem. Larkspur is extremely ethylene sensitive; keep it away from ripening fruit.

Laurel

Vase Life: 14+ days

Harvest when the leaves are leathery to the touch.

Lavatera

Vase Life: 7 to 10 days

Harvest when just a few flowers have opened on the stem.

Leucojum

Vase Life: 7 to 10 days

Harvest when two-thirds of the flowers have unfurled.

Lilac (*Syringa* species)

Vase Life: 5 to 6 days

Harvest when one-half to three-quarters of the flowers on the bloom cluster are open, and immediately remove most or all of the leaves. Woody.

Lily

Vase Life: 7 to 10 days

Harvest when the buds are colored and the bottom flower is just beginning to open. Remove pollen anthers as the flowers mature to prevent staining.

Lisianthus (*Eustoma grandiflorum*)

Vase Life: 10 to 14 days

Harvest when there are 2 or 3 open blooms on a spray.

Love-in-a-mist (*Nigella* species)

Vase Life: 7 days

Harvest flowers when they are three-quarters open, or harvest pods when formed. Dry by hanging upside down in a warm, dark place for 2 to 3 weeks.

Love-in-a-puff vine (*Cardiospermum halicacabum*)

Vase Life: 5 to 7 days

Harvest stems once they are covered in little green lanterns. It's especially wilt prone, so cut during the coolest part of the day. **Wimpy.**

Lupine

Vase Life: 7 days

Harvest when the bottom florets are just opening.

Marigold (*Tagetes* species)

Vase Life: 7 to 10 days

Harvest when the flowers are about half open, and strip off most of the foliage.

Mignonette (*Reseda* species)

Vase Life: 5 to 7 days

Harvest when the bottom one-third of the flowers on a spire open, or let them bloom and pick after the seedpods mature. Stems are delicate and must be picked with care.

Millet (*Pennisetum* species)

Vase Life: 14+ days

Harvest any time after the heads have emerged from the sheaf, but before color fades and they begin to drop little seeds. Can also be dried and used indefinitely.

Mint

Vase Life: 7 days

Harvest once the stems have become firm and are no longer floppy when wiggled. Strip the lower third of foliage. **Wimpy.**

Mock orange (*Philadelphus*)

Vase Life: 5 to 10 days

Harvest when the flower buds are just opening. For foliage, pick once the leaves are leathery and firm. **Woody.**

Nandina

Vase Life: 10 to 15 days

For blooms, harvest when the white flowers are still in bud; for berries, pick when the clusters start to color. Foliage can be harvested as soon as it becomes leathery.

Narcissus (includes daffodils and paperwhites)

Vase Life: 7 days

Harvest when blooms look like a goose neck and have not yet opened. Place stems in separate bucket to rest for 3 to 4 hours to release sap. Do not recut stems after treatment. **Sappy.**

Nasturtium (*Tropaeolum majus*)

Vase Life: 7 to 10 days

Harvest the flowers just as they are opening. If using entire vines, harvest when the foliage becomes leathery or firm to the touch.

Nerine (*Nerine bowdenii*)

Vase Life: 7+ days

Harvest when the flowers are one-half to two-thirds open.

Ninebark (*Physocarpus opulifolius*)

Vase Life: 10 to 14 days

Harvest when the foliage is leathery and the tips are no longer floppy. For springtime flowers, harvest when the buds are colored but not yet open, and strip the bottom third of the stem. **Woody.**

Orach (*Atriplex hortensis*)

Vase Life: 7 to 14 days

Can be harvested in the foliage stage or once seedpods have formed. Seeded stems require no special treatment. **Wimpy.**

Oregano

Vase Life: 7 to 10 days

Harvest at any stage, whether in flower or when seed heads have formed. **Dirty.**

Orlaya

Vase Life: 7 to 10 days

Harvest when the flowers are half to fully open. If harvested earlier, the stems tend to wilt. **Wimpy.**

Pansy

Vase Life: 5 to 7 days

Harvest when the flowers are starting to open. Stems lengthen over time.

Parsley (*Petroselinum crispum*)

Vase Life: 7+ days

Harvest the leaves once they are firm. Flowers appear on second year's growth. Pick after seedpods mature.

Passion vine (*Passiflora* species)

Vase Life: 5 to 7 days

Harvest when the stems and leaves have become firm. Handle tendrils gently.

Pea (*Pisum sativum*)

Vase Life: 5 to 7 days

Harvest when the pods are brightly colored, taking care when handling delicate vines.

Peony

Vase Life: 5 to 7 days

For the longest vase life, harvest when the buds feel like a soft marshmallow when squeezed. Can be stored out of water in the cooler for up to 2 weeks. Recut and place in water before using.

Pepper tree (*Schinus* species)

Vase Life: 7 to 10 days

Harvest when the berry clusters are just beginning to color.

Phlox

Vase Life: 5 to 7 days

Harvest when just a few flowers are open, no more than half.

Pieris

Vase Life: 7 to 10 days

Harvest branches while the flowers are still in bud, before they have fully opened. **Woody.**

Pincushion flower (*Scabiosa*)

Vase Life: 7 to 10 days

Harvest when the flowers are still in the bud stage or just beginning to open.

Poinsettia (*Euphorbia pulcherrima*)

Vase Life: 14+ days

Harvest when the flower bracts have started to color and before the tiny central flowers have completely opened. Remove green foliage. Use caution and wear gloves; the sap is irritating to skin and eyes. **Sappy.**

Pokeweed (*Phytolacca americana*)

Vase Life: 14+ days

Harvest foliage and mature flowers that have turned to green seedpods or purple berries. All parts of the plant are considered toxic, so wear gloves when handling and keep it away from children and pets.

Porcelain berry (*Ampelopsis glandulosa*)

Vase Life: 7 to 10 days

Harvest in autumn when the berries are blue; remove foliage so the fruit is more visible.

Privet (*Ligustrum* species)

Vase Life: 2 to 3 weeks

Harvest branches with leathery leaves or wait for the blue-black berries in the winter. **Woody.**

Pussy willow (*Salix* species)

Vase Life: 14+ days

Harvest branches when the catkins have swelled and the bud scales have dropped off. You can dry stems with full catkins before any yellow pollen has appeared, standing the stems upright in a cool room. **Woody.**

Quince (*Chaenomeles* species)

Vase Life: 7 to 10 days

Harvest stems when the flower buds are swollen and colored. **Woody.**

Ranunculus

Vase Life: 7 to 10 days

Cut when the buds are colored and squishy like a marshmallow, but not completely open. Can be picked when more mature but will be more fragile during transport.

Raspberry

Vase Life: 7 to 14 days

For berries, harvest before the fruit fully ripens. For foliage, harvest when leathery and firm. **Woody.**

Red-leaf hibiscus (*Hibiscus acetosella*)

Vase Life: 7 days

Harvest when the foliage is leathery and the tips are no longer floppy. **Wimpy.**

Rockrose (*Cistus × obtusifolius*)
Vase Life: 14+ days

For flowers, harvest when the buds are colored but before they've fully opened. For foliage, cut at any time.

Rose
Vase Life: 5 days

Harvest when the flowers are one-third to one-half open. If not arranging right away, store in a cooler until ready to use. **Woody.**

Rose hips
Vase Life: 14+ days

Harvest when the hips are colored but before they start to shrivel. Remove all leaves. **Woody.**

Rosemary (*Rosmarinus officinalis*)
Vase Life: 7 to 10 days

Harvest at any stage throughout the season. **Woody.**

Russian sage (*Perovskia*)
Vase Life: 7 to 10 days

Harvest when the flowers are at least three-quarters open; bracts can be used after the flowers drop.

Salvia
Vase Life: 7 to 10 days

Harvest when the flowers are at least three-quarters open; bracts can be used after the flowers drop.

Sanguisorba
Vase Life: 7 days

Harvest when the catkin-like blooms have colored. The foliage smells like cucumber.

Scented geranium (*Pelargonium* species)
Vase Life: 7 days

Wait to harvest until the plants have matured enough for the stems to harden a bit. It's wilt prone, so be sure to cut during the coolest part of the day and remove foliage from the lower half of the stems. **Wimpy.**

Sea holly (*Eryngium* species)
Vase Life: 7 to 10 days

Harvest when the flowers turn blue but before pollen shows. Remove most of the foliage, as it will yellow prematurely. This is a unique textural filler, but it has a very unpleasant smell.

Sedum (*Sedum spectabile*)
Vase Life: 14+ days

Harvest any time after flower heads form. It has a long harvest window, from early summer to autumn.

Shiso (*Perilla frutescens*)
Vase Life: 7 to 14 days

Harvest when the foliage has become thick and the stems are woody, or any time after a flower spike begins to emerge. Wimpy.

Smokebush (*Cotinus* species)
Vase Life: 7 days

For flowers, harvest anytime after the cloud-like blooms are visible. For foliage, harvest when firm. Woody.

Snapdragon (*Antirrhinum majus*)
Vase Life: 7 to 10 days

Harvest when just the bottom 2 or 3 flowers are open.

Snowberry (*Symphoricarpos* species)
Vase Life: 7 to 10 days

Harvest berried stems while the berries are plump, before they fully ripen and soften. For foliage, harvest after the leaves become leathery. Woody.

Soapwort (*Saponaria officinalis*)
Vase Life: 7 days

Harvest when one-third of the flowers on a stem are open. Wimpy.

Solomon's seal (*Polygonatum* species)
Vase Life: 7 to 10 days

Harvest foliage at ground level in early spring before the flowers appear or when 3 or 4 blooms have opened.

Spirea
Vase Life: 7 to 14 days

Harvest when the flower buds have colored or as the first florets are opening. Long branches should be cut with no more than one-third of the flowers open. For foliage, harvest after the flowers have dropped and the leaves are leathery. Woody.

Stock (*Matthiola incana*)
Vase Life: 7 to 10 days

Harvest when half the florets on a stem are open. Change the water often to avoid cabbage-y smell. Dirty.

Strawflower (*Bracteantha bracteata*)
Vase Life: 7+ days

Harvest when the flowers are half open and before they are pollinated. To dry, remove foliage and hang upside down in a warm, dark place until firm.

Sunflower (*Helianthus annuus*)
Vase Life: 7 to 10 days

Harvest as soon as the first petals on a bloom start to lift off of the central disk. Strip three-quarters of the leaves from the stem.

Sweet Annie (*Artemisia annua*)
Vase Life: 7 days

Harvest before the golden flowers open, to avoid pollen shed. The foliage has a strong scent and is an allergen for some. Dry by hanging upside down in a warm, dark place for 2 weeks.

Sweet pea (*Lathyrus odoratus*)
Vase Life: 4 to 5 days

Harvest when there are at least 2 unopened flowers at the tip of a stem. It's especially important to use flower food.

Sweet rocket (*Hesperis matronalis*)
Vase Life: 5 to 7 days

Harvest when the first few flowers on a stem begin to open. Stems continue to grow after being cut, so keep this in mind when arranging.

Sweet William (*Dianthus barbatus*)
Vase Life: 14+ days

Harvest when 2 or 3 flowers on a stem are open.

Tickseed (*Coreopsis lanceolata*)
Vase Life: 7 days

Harvest when two-thirds of the flowers on the stem have opened. **Wimpy.**

Tomato
Vase Life: 4 to 5 days

Harvest after all of the fruit has developed on a cluster, but before fully colored. Remove all the leaves, as they will wilt.

Tuberose (*Polianthes tuberosa*)
Vase Life: 7 to 10 days

Harvest when 2 or 3 florets on a stem are open and the rest are showing color. Can be picked when more mature, but ideally, when no more than half of the florets are open.

Tulip

Vase Life: 7 to 10 days

Harvest when flowers are in bud, with a hint of color showing on the outer petals. For extended storage, leave the bulb attached and store upright out of water in a cooler up to 2 weeks. Remove bulb to use flower.

Viburnum

Vase Life: 7 to 10 days

For snowball types, harvest when blooms are green. For all other flowering types, harvest when one-third of florets are open. Harvest berries before they fully ripen and become soft. Woody.

Vine maple (*Acer circinatum*)

Vase Life: 7 days

Harvest after the leaves become leathery. Woody.

Wild sorrel (*Rumex acetosella*)

Vase Life: 5 days

Harvest when the seed heads are mature and not droopy.

Witch Hazel (*Hamamelis* species)

Vase Life: 5 to 9 days

Harvest the flowers when the buds are just starting to open. Woody.

Yarrow (*Achillea millefolium*)

Vase Life: 5 to 7 days

Harvest when at least three-quarters of the florets are open on the flower heads and pollen is showing. If picked too early, the flowers will wilt and not recover. Dirty.

Zinnia (*Zinnia elegans*)

Vase Life: 7 days

Use the "wiggle test": grab the stem about 8 in (20 cm) down from the flower and gently shake it. If the stem is droopy or bends, don't cut yet. If the stem is stiff and remains erect, it is ready to harvest. Do not put in the cooler. Dirty.

CROSS-REFERENCED INGREDIENTS

Barley (see Grains)

Cedar (see Evergreens)

Cypress (see Evergreens)

Daffodil (see Narcissus)

Hemlock (see Evergreens)

Northern sea oats (see Grasses)

Oats (see Grains)

Paperwhites (see Narcissus)

Pennycress (see Cress)

Rat-tail radish (see Grains)

Not a true grain but treated as one in this book's bouquet

Rye (see Grains)

Viola (see Pansy)

Yew (see Evergreens)

Resources

The following sources and supplies are among my favorites.

DIRECTORIES OF LOCAL FLOWER FARMERS

Association of Specialty Cut Flower Growers
www.ascfg.org
This association has an online directory featuring their many members, all of whom are passionate about local, seasonal flowers.

Floret's Farmer-Florist Collective
www.floretflowers.com/directory
Our free online directory features over a thousand (and growing) flower farmers, floral designers, and farmer-florists who are committed to growing, buying, and promoting local flowers. Every member of the collective has pledged to highlight local, seasonal flowers and use sustainable growing and business practices whenever possible. I encourage you to connect with and support these committed, passionate artisans in your community.

Slow Flowers
www.slowflowers.com
This online directory features floral designers, markets, and farmers who are committed to using and providing North America–grown flowers.

VASES

Campo de' Fiori
www.campodefiori.com
Specialty source for terra-cotta pots and planters. Retail and wholesale pricing.

Farmhouse Pottery
www.farmhousepottery.com
Handcrafted pottery that will stand the test of time.

Floral Supply Syndicate
www.fss.com
Vast selection of simple and affordable glass vases in bulk. Retail and wholesale pricing.

Frances Palmer Pottery
www.francespalmerpottery.com
Artisan ceramic vessels by famed East Coast potter Frances Palmer.

Jamali Garden
www.jamaligarden.com
Unusual and affordable vases available in bulk. Retail and wholesale pricing.

Object & Totem
www.objectandtotem.com
Ceramic studio producing one-of-a-kind vases and limited-edition vessels.

SUPPLIES

46 & Spruce

www.46spruce.com

Retail source for Holly Heider Chapple pillows and eggs.

Eco Fresh Bouquet

www.ecofreshbouquet.com

Floral hydration stem wrap, excellent for large-scale installations and keeping hand-tied bouquets fresh.

Floral Supply Syndicate

www.fss.com

Extensive inventory, including floral and waterproof tape, straight pins, Oasis floral adhesive, jute twine, Oasis rustic wire, 22- and 24-gauge wire, paper-covered wire, paddle wire, wire wreath frames, floral adhesive clay, and pin frogs.

Floret Farm

www.floretflowers.com

Flower snips and pruners, custom aprons, hairpin frogs, and pin frogs. We also carry seeds and bulbs of many of the varieties shown in this book.

Jamali Garden

www.jamaligarden.com

Flower-arranging supplies, including flower preservative, floral tape/stem wrap, Oasis waterproof floral tape, jute and cotton twine, bind wire, paper-covered wire, rose thorn stripper, water tubes, and floral adhesive clay (Sure-Stik).

Jan's Jewelry Supplies

www.jansjewels.com

Brass cuffs and a wide variety of jewelry bases.

May Arts

www.mayarts.com

Large selection of ribbon, including affordable silk in many colors and widths. Wholesale pricing available.

Michaels

www.michaels.com

Wide variety of crafting supplies, including jute twine, paper-covered wire, paddle wire, wire wreath frames, and chicken wire.

Midori

www.midoriribbon.com

Extensive collection of silk and double-faced satin ribbon.

Save On Crafts

www.save-on-crafts.com

Floral wire, paddle wire, wire wreath frames, vases, and flower frogs at affordable prices.

Silk & Willow

www.silkandwillow.com

Our favorite source for plant-dyed silk ribbon.

Syndicate Sales

www.syndicatesales.com

Holly Heider Chapple eggs and pillows, chicken wire, plastic buckets, and vases. Wholesale only.

303

Acknowledgments

ERIN BENZAKEIN

Along this journey, I have been blessed by so many incredible people who have taken the time to share their gifts, talents, and wisdom with me. My hope is that I can repay their generosity by sharing all that I know. Chris, thank you for always supporting my crazy ideas and for capturing the beauty and magic of our life. I love you millions and billions. Mom, thank you for always reminding me that I have all the words I need to tell the story and to keep going even when I want to give up. Elora and Jasper, thank you for always believing in what I'm trying to do, even when it seems nuts. You guys are the best. Jill, can you believe we actually got to write a book together? I am so lucky to have had you by my side through everything. You made this massive project into a fun and joy-filled experience. I can't wait to see what we do next! Julie Chai, thank you for being the voice of reason and for your constant support and encouragement. I am so thankful we found each other. Rachel Hiles and the Chronicle Books team, thank you for so enthusiastically supporting this project and helping us bring it to life. I hope that there are many more books to come. Heartfelt thanks to Leslie Jonath and Leslie Stoker for your wise counsel and unwavering faith in this project. Massive gratitude to Susan King for helping define the scope of this beautiful book and for getting it into as many hands as possible. To the Floret workshop team, thank you for all of the love and support you poured into helping each and every student find their way. Ariella Chezar, thank you for taking a chance on me. Your kindness and generosity changed my life. Amy Merrick, thank you for helping me see what was there all along. Your friendship opened my eyes and set me on a new path. Sue Prutting, thank you for helping me find the courage to face my fears and for your unwavering support during the early workshop years. Frances Palmer, having your beautiful work grace the pages of this book is such a dream come true. Your encouragement along the way has been priceless. Sarah Ryhanen and Nicolette Camille Owen, you ladies sure set the bar high. Huge props for always pushing the limits and showing the world what's possible. Joanna Gaines, thank you for believing in our story and for all of your support. Martha Stewart, your hard work and dedication paved the way for us all. Thank you for helping put Floret on the map. Jan Johnson, thank you for coming to my rescue when I needed it most and for blessing me with your endless patience and guidance in those early days. Jana Belisle, not only did you teach me how to garden, but you also taught me how to find magic in the smallest details. I'm still reaping the benefits of the time I spent with you. Huge thanks to Team Floret for holding down the fort and caring so deeply about the work we're fortunate enough to do. Nina Foster, my first flower friend, thank you for helping me not feel crazy about how much I love flowers. Thank you to all the wonderful farmers who shared their flowers and opened up their fields to this project. Your generosity is greatly appreciated. Lastly, to all of the Floret fans and readers, thank you for so eagerly sharing your dreams and desires with us. This book is for you!

JILL JORGENSEN

I am so happy to thank the following people for helping realize this long-standing dream. Erin, thank you for sharing your ideas with me. I value the teaching and learning that we get to do together every day. Your vision, passion, and determination are inspiring. We've created a lot of amazing things around your dining room table, and I'm so proud of what we put out into the world. Chris, thank you for your commitment to teaching yourself new things, for your endless patience, and for capturing this entire project; it was no small feat. To the Floret workshop students and team, thank you for being the catalyst for this book; those flower-filled weekends will always be the most beautiful of my life. To Team Floret, thank you for supporting us so we could tuck away and write, and for the love and care you pour in. Susan Studer King, thank you for helping lay the foundation for this book and for being the ultimate cheerleader along the way. Without you, we wouldn't have been able to take on this massive project. To all the Floret fans and readers for sharing the love of flowers: The world is a better, more beautiful place because of you. Thank you to Rachel Hiles at Chronicle for being an awesome communicator and for being so easy to work with. To agents Leslie Jonath and Leslie Stoker, thank you for your wise counsel and great enthusiasm for every project we do. Editor Julie Chai, you are a total pro. Thank you for taking such good care of this book and for your excitement every step of the way. To my husband, Joel, thank you for your steady-as-she-goes nature and your ability to figure anything out, and for being super dad. We are lucky to have you. To my village, thank you for caring for our children on already long days and for loving them as your own. It would be a lonely road without you. My friends Caite, Ann, and Christina: Thank you for your humor and your smarts, and for holding the standard for ladies who get after it. Michelle Jordan, thank you for giving me my first job in flowers and for showing me that 'Casa Blanca' lilies really are the ultimate luxury. Thank you to Jeff and Katie for your support of my work and for taking such great care of the kids. To my grandparents, George and Katy, thank you for creating such a magical world for Anne and me to explore, and for getting our hands in the dirt; we miss you terribly. To my parents, Tom and Sue, sister Anne, and the entire Melton family: Thank you for demonstrating hard work, for passing down your quick wit, and for showing me how to value and appreciate the written word—all these gifts have served me well. Lastly, to Cora and Felix, my hope is that you find something that lights you up and have the patience and resolve to see where it guides you. I'm lucky to be your mama.

JULIE CHAI

This book has been one of my favorite collaborations yet, and I'm grateful to so many who've helped me along in both big and small ways. Erin Benzakein, I know how much of yourself you poured into this book and how much it means to you. Thank you for once again trusting me to help tell your story. Your sincerity, willingness to do whatever it takes to get things right, and generous spirit are second to none. Jill Jorgensen, thank you for your graciousness, dedication, and positivity every step of the way. Getting to know you has been icing on the cake. Leslie Jonath, your eternal optimism and staunch support mean so much to me. I am grateful for your friendship and wisdom. Thank you to Leslie Stoker for your thoughtful guidance. Rachel Hiles and the team at Chronicle Books, thank you for your collaborative spirit and pouring so much creativity into this book. Mom and Dad, your enthusiasm for life, love of learning, and appreciation of the natural world inspire me always. Thank you for letting me loose to play in the mud, climb trees, and make big messes. My George, you are the voice of reason and help me stay rooted. Thank you for keeping our home filled with laughter and for your unfailing encouragement to grow whatever interests me, both in our garden and in life. Our Ellis—harvester, bouquet maker, collector of rocks, twigs, and lizard skins—watching you learn, grow, and discover the world is the thrill of a lifetime. Thank you for making every day brighter.

CHRIS BENZAKEIN

Erin, the love of my life, we finally got to do a book together, just like we always dreamed. I love you millions and billions. Chérie, thank you for always reminding me that I'm golden. Elora and Jasper, I love you both dearly. Jill, thanks for keeping us laughing even when our plate is way too full!

305

Index

306

309

310